To Rome with the Homeless

To Rome with the Homeless

NINE STORIES OF HOPE

TANYA CANGELOSI   ELISE ANN ALLEN

Our Sunday Visitor
Huntington, Indiana

Our Sunday Visitor Publishing Division
Our Sunday Visitor, Inc.
200 Noll Plaza
Huntington, IN 46750
www.osv.com
1-800-348-2440

ISBN: 978-1-68192-795-4 (Inventory No. T2665)
1. RELIGION—Christian Living—Inspirational.
2. RELIGION—Christian Living—Social Issues.
3. RELIGION—Christianity—Catholic.

eISBN: 978-1-68192-796-1
LCCN: 2022938875

Cover design: Tyler Ottinger
Cover art: Adobe Stock
Interior design: Amanda Falk

PRINTED IN THE UNITED STATES OF AMERICA

This book is dedicated to my goddaughter
Naomi O'Loughlin.

In loving memory of my mother, Leta (Turner) Butler,
who never gave up on me, and DeAnne Anderson,
who loved unconditionally and whose care and
generosity gave me a second chance at life.

This book is also dedicated to John, without whose
support it would not have been possible.

Contents

Content Advisory
Please note that while this is fundamentally a story of hope, *To Rome with the Homeless* features stories of people who grew up in difficult situations, and therefore contains content related to drug and alcohol abuse, sexual assault/rape, and suicide, which some readers may find difficult.

Preface

In 2009, while interning for the Air Force over the summer, I found myself attending Holy Protection of the Mother of God, an Eastern-rite church in Denver, Colorado. There I had the good fortune to encounter and become friends with Tanya Cangelosi. I discovered in her and in Holy Protection's pastor two people with a tangible zeal for service to the poor. It was an enlightening experience to hear their stories of a simple ministry in the form of small acts of kindness, and a lesson I tried to take home and to heart. So it was a privilege the following year for my first real act as a newly licensed attorney to be to help Tanya found the Denver Homeless Ministry, the organization through which she brought the people in this book to Rome.

From the outset, the DHM intended "to serve the homeless by seeing them as our equals and friends." That intent was put into the organization's founding documents, and it reflects the spirit of mutual respect that Tanya so delightfully embodies, and which clearly grew so naturally from her first chance encounter with the homeless on the steps of Colorado's capitol. Not knowing that the lady with whom she was speaking was homeless, Tanya was simply at ease having a conversation and being friendly. The same was true as she met more people in the same way, ultimately not discovering that her friends were homeless until one mentioned she was going to the 16th Street Mall to ask for spare change or leftovers. Tanya had seen her friends not as they were labeled, but simply as they were, and in that light approached them from a position of equality.

Because she approaches the homeless as equals and friends, and not just as charity cases, we may begin to understand how Tanya could respond to God's call to start the Roman trips which are the backbone of this book. As she admits, some people may ask, "Why spend all that money, just for one person?" However, how many of us would not want to travel to Rome with friends or family, and offer the assistance to make that possible? Most of us would, but lacking that reciprocity of friendship, ministry to the homeless becomes less comprehensible. Certainly, the sort of extravagant friendship that invites and helps a friend travel with you abroad becomes baffling.

Yet the friendships Tanya has struck up, and which feature in this book, are ones in which there is mutual exchange. *To Rome with the Homeless* shows that Tree, Shyla, and the other individuals Tanya brought to Rome not only received, but gave as well. They gave in tangible ways, such as when Tree assisted with the Missionaries of Charity, and in intangible ones, such as the example they set for those living on the street who doubt life can be different. The surety of the latter has been an important basis for my own continuing support of this mission. But you, the reader, are a beneficiary as well. In each chapter you will discover not only how the beneficiaries of Tanya's love for the poor benefited from the life-changing experience of a Roman pilgrimage, but also how the experience of going on pilgrimage with them changed Tanya and helped cast new light on the Catholic Faith and its exemplars. Now you too can grow from these experiences, and perhaps bring that same Christian love to others.

—Stephen Braunlich
Former DHM board member

Foreword

I first heard the extraordinary story of Tanya Cangelosi on a sunset cruise in the Florida Keys. There — in a pre-pandemic complacency amid every comfort, attending a wedding full of hopes and dreams for the future — Tanya revealed her harrowing, yet inspiring personal journey, and her mission to help others find a path from despair to hope.

As an art historian, specializing in the Baroque, my business is beauty. Paintings, sculptures, and dazzling structures create a cornice of loveliness that can shut out the gritty reality of life. How could our two worlds ever collide? Thanks to Tanya's unique vision, however, a Venn diagram began to appear. Tanya has not only lived through horrific ugliness in her life, but she has also delved into the depths of human brokenness, and she has been able to find beauty where very few can. In her ministry to Denver's homeless, among whom addiction, violence, and abuse are rife, Tanya has witnessed the lovely and loving light of redemption, as she, following the injunction of Pope Francis, ventures "to the peripheries, not only geographically, but also the existential peripheries: the mystery of sin, of pain, of injustice, of ignorance and indifference to religion, of intellectual currents, and of all forms of misery."*

In this book, Tanya's thumbnail "tours" of the centers where Denver's homeless congregate are chilling. From terrifying tunnels where drugs and violence reign, to the sparse refuges from icy Colorado winters, to rats, vermin, and their accompanying diseases, it would seem that light could never enter into such impenetrable darkness. When she recounts a random act of kindness or a slight success, it feels like a sunbeam on a frosty morning, and one realizes that a kind word, or recognition of their human dignity to the marginalized people of the streets can be as important as food and blankets.

Faith framed Tanya's vision to help lead souls out of their tunnels, both literal and figurative, and that faith shines forth in every page of the book. It is the underpinning of her Denver Homeless Ministry; it is the light that leads her into the shadowy complexities of these lives, and it is the lens that allows her to see beyond the rags and destitution to the child of God within. Looking through her eyes has taught me a different way of seeing; one I never would have learned from my studies. In the words of Pope Francis, "In the shoes of the other, we learn to have a great capacity for understanding, for getting to know difficult situations."† Tanya goes a step further: She helps the reader to recognize the beauty within.

This book tells nine stories, stories that would go unnoticed

---

*Pope Francis, Message to the Participants in the Meeting for Friendship among Peoples, Vatican. va.

† Pope Francis, from a February 28 interview in *Scarp de'tenis* magazine, as quoted in "Pope Francis Gives Interview to 'Homeless' Magazine," Herald Malaysia Online, March 1, 2017, http://www .heraldmalaysia.com/news/pope-francis-gives-interview-to-homeless-magazine/34974/1.

by most, of people suffering on the streets, both urban and spiritual vagrants. Tanya holds up these individual and unique works of art, the fruit of a collective effort to forge a new persona out of what most perceive as the shapeless huddled figures of the street. Listening to her on that boat, it seemed that these stories needed to be heard by many more than just a few privileged revelers. Enter Elise Harris Allen, whose wedding we were attending. She and Tanya had been friends for years and Elise had played an integral part of the Rome experience for these pilgrims. Elise, a seasoned Rome reporter with a great sense of storytelling, took these amazing tales and gave them structure and order, the essence of art.

The Venn diagram of Tanya's work and mine converges in Rome, where she has brought each of her seven charges over the years. Rome is a city of saints and sinners, of Peter the prince of the apostles and Nero the mad emperor. It also once ruled the world but has also been sacked, burnt, abandoned, and shaken to its foundations by earthquakes. The head of an empire and the capitol of Christendom, Rome has seen it all, and has an effect on all who walk her timeless streets.

It is a city of triumph, like the remarkable story of Clarissa in these pages; it is a city of setbacks, like those of Shyla, Tanya's most challenging pilgrim. Rome's layers contain so many human stories, it is difficult not to feel at home. Its Baroque cornices, Piazza Navona, Spanish Steps, and St. Peter's Square are like theatrical stages set throughout the city. In these places, open to all and embellished with glorious statues, fountains, flowers, and churches, visitors and denizens are invited to feel like actors, true protagonists of their own lives. It is a magnificent stage set, where all are welcome to strut or fret, as the case may be, and a reminder that it is our own actions and choices that define us, as an artist's decisions about what to add or subtract make a work of art.

Coaching the multitude of "actors" in the Eternal City are the ubiquitous saints: men and women whose extraordinary "performances" have gained them a place in heaven. Tanya feels the proximity of the saints, from St. Margaret of Cortona to St. Benedict Joseph Labre, and perceives their similarities with her charges, undoubtedly a factor in her success. In the culmination of her trips, she brings her pilgrims to see the pope in the embrace of the enormous Vatican piazza, where she joins their immediate struggles and challenges to those overcome by the saints celebrated in the 140 statues arranged around the colonnade, and together, they receive the blessing of the successor of Saint Peter.

Rome may have its up and downs, but in *To Rome with the Homeless*, Tanya and Elise make a compelling argument that it is still the *caput mundi* of conversion.

—Elizabeth Lev
Art historian, author, lecturer, and tour guide

Introduction

When I talk to people about the work of the Denver Homeless Ministry (DHM), they always want to hear more about our annual pilgrimages to Rome. Each year for the past eight years, I've asked God to help me choose one person to bring with me to see the Eternal City, to take in its beauty and to give them a "jump start" on a new life.

"Why spend all that money, just for one person?" is a question I get a lot. "How can you afford it? And what difference does it make?" Of course, the Gospels are full of similar stories: the Good Samaritan, who put himself in debt to tend to the needs of a stranger he found by the side of the road; the determined shepherd who left his entire flock unguarded in order to reach that one lost sheep; the unnamed woman who poured out an expensive bottle of ointment on the feet of Jesus, deaf to the outraged cries of Judas that the expensive oils could have been put to better use.

But I don't tell them these stories. That's not really my thing. Instead, I tell them about people like Katie Henke.

Eight years ago, Katie probably would have laughed if someone told her that one day she would be in Rome staring at Michelangelo's *Last Judgment*, a cornerstone of High Renaissance art widely regarded as among the greatest masterpieces of all time. Back then, Katie was addicted to meth, struggling with mental illness, and drinking heavily every day.

Yet there she was, admiring the main altar of the Sistine Chapel, and the detailed frescoes depicting scenes of God's creation of the world from the biblical Book of Genesis. Surprisingly, it was not the beauty of the chapel, the magnificence of the art it held, or the history surrounding her that moved Katie most in that moment. What caught her attention was the priest standing beside the main altar, hushing boisterous tourists, and reminding them that they were in a sacred place. He didn't seem to mind when a couple of us came up and asked if we could go to confession.

Katie watched as I went first. Then, as one of our chaperones stood up, Katie asked if she could go up too, even though she wasn't Catholic. The chaperone told Katie that it was fine if she wanted to go talk to the priest, and to get in line if she wanted to. So, to our surprise, Katie did. She came back to where we were sitting a short time later, misty-eyed, saying what the priest told her had brought her to tears. Sitting inside the Sistine Chapel during a dream trip to Rome, Katie's heart and mind in that moment were back in Denver, Colorado, with her five-year-old daughter, Anastasia. She told the priest she didn't think she was a good mother because of her past and some of the things she had done in life.

She half-expected that he would tell her to leave, but he didn't. He told her that she was a good mother, and not to be so hard on herself; that she was doing her best, that she loved her daughter, and needed to give herself a break. As I listened to Katie tell us this story, I could see God acting in her life, and I was humbled to play a part in her experience during this trip to Rome. I wanted her to be reminded of who she was as a beloved daughter of God, and to learn to see herself as God sees her.

It was a moving experience for all of us who were there. Katie left the chapel that day with her head a little higher, and I went home thanking God that, once again, he had given me a vision for coming here, and for giving people like Katie an opportunity to see themselves — and to see him in a whole new light; to see that good things really do happen for those who are willing to take that courageous, life-changing step toward mercy.

Mercy on the Streets

Of course, you don't have to go all the way to Rome to learn about mercy. I found God's school of mercy on the streets of Denver, Colorado. In fact, if you want to know about mercy, there is perhaps no greater education than the one to be found on the streets among the homeless.

Not long after my husband and I divorced, I moved to Denver and rented a studio apartment on Capitol Hill. I didn't know anyone, and in the evenings after getting home from work I would eat dinner and then head over to the steps of the Capitol to read or just sit on the hill looking over the parks, daydreaming and saying hello to the many people who walked by. It was in these moments that I found unexpected friendship in the middle of my loneliness.

One day while I was sitting on the steps of the Capitol feeling sorry for myself, a lady came up and sat on the steps with me. We started chatting about the weather, the park, people, nothing of importance — just being friendly. After a few weeks of sitting outside, we had a group of six or more who just gathered to chat.

I didn't find out until later that my new friends were homeless! It was the simple fellowship I was craving. I didn't have to work at being liked, they just simply liked me.

And the thing was, I liked them, too.

The Darkness and the Glory

Oftentimes people are not on the streets for the reasons you'd think, and in most cases they don't want to be there. They come from broken homes, tough childhoods, and families where drugs, alcohol, and abuse are the norm. Not all parents are bad, nor are all children bad, but there are many bad situations that people just don't know how to deal with, and people often fall through the cracks.

Other homeless people are veterans who never learned to cope with trauma after combat, struggling to hold down a job and turning to substance abuse to escape from their bitter realities. Many of the vets I met on the streets were alcoholics. They were also some of the most loving and caring people you could ever want to have around you; they just didn't know how to cope. Many had been living on the streets for so long they didn't even know where to go to get help and some had stopped wanting it, so the best we could do is make sure they were fed and had warm socks.

I often ran into children, too — children who had escaped "the system" that should have helped them, and parents who were themselves so broken that they were unable to tend to their children's needs. My friend Arkansas, for example, got hooked on meth and heroin because of his mother, who taught him how to deal and later served as his supplier. Melanie, one of the women you'll meet later in this book, ran away from home because she grew tired of having to put her father to bed every night because he was drunk and her mother was passed out. Another young gay man was stabbed by his father, but eventually went back home to care for him when his father got cancer.

I encountered so many young ones on the streets during my time working with homeless people in Denver, children that the system had utterly failed. I especially remember two street children, "Harry" (age eleven) and "George" (age nine). Harry had run away from his family in Texas, hitchhiked all the way to Colorado and was placed in a juvenile facility where he said he was being abused. To prove it, Harry showed me bruises and cuts. I convinced him to let me talk to the police, who would be coming to pick him up, to see if they could help me work something out. The cop I spoke to was very accommodating. He looked at each of the boy's bruises and said he would do his job. I could only hope he would keep that promise.

Harry's friend George had come from a sad place, too. George's parents were running a meth lab and they were afraid to get caught with a child in their home, since it would qualify as child endangerment (whereas just having a meth lab would result in more of a slap on the wrist).

This little boy told me that his family still got a social security check for him, but he never saw any of it. It took a lot to talk him into going back into protective custody ("the system"). At the time, they were staying in a sort of holding place that houses kids until they are either placed in foster care or adopted. To get George to go back, I promised him that I would do everything in my power to try to help him. I didn't know if I would be able to keep that promise, but I was determined to try.

When the day came to turn him over to the police, we walked up to the state capitol, away from the rest of the homeless population, to wait for the police to come and pick him up. A security guard waited with us, and at one point George looked up at him and said, "Would you please be my daddy?" I cannot explain the look on the guard's face. He looked at me with huge eyes brimming with tears and a look of such sadness that I had to turn away. I had no idea what to say. Finally, this guard told George that he had a family, and it just wouldn't be possible. I never saw George again. One of the hardest parts of working on the streets is that you don't always have closure.

There are some "glory moments," though; times when we were able to do something to help change the course of a life. A few years ago, a young man asked for a suit. We gave him one, and then he seemed to disappear. We hadn't seen him in quite some time, but one day when we were doing outreach, this same young man ran across the street to give me a hug and tell me he just got off work and that he couldn't have done it without the help he got from the Denver Homeless Ministry. That's why we do what we do. The Lord doesn't always allow us to see the fruits of our labors, but when he does it's a joyful blessing.

In most cases, what we do involves reminding those we meet of their value, their goodness, their personal dignity through what Pope Francis called "the culture of encounter." Through those encounters of mercy, some believed us and took the steps to change their situation. We can't do that for them, but we can love them into that next place, by giving them back their dignity.

One time when my family was in town for a short visit, as we were walking down the street, a middle-aged gentleman approached me and said, "I don't want or need anything, I just want to know if I can give you a hug." I said yes and hugged him back, and then he said, "I know you don't know who I am, but we all know who you are, and I just want to say thank you for all you do for us."

You don't get many of those glory moments on the streets, but when you do, it just about melts your heart!

Looking with the Eyes of Christ

Many of the people I met on the streets of Denver have never seen or felt unconditional love. As Christians, we have received the mercy of God in so many ways and are called to be that mercy to others we encounter each day, whether on the streets of Denver or in our own backyard. It can be uncomfortable to look someone in the eye, knowing that they might ask you for something. Yet sometimes what they need even more than money is a simple acknowledgment of their humanity — just looking that person in the eye and saying hello.

In the Acts of the Apostles, the apostle Peter met a lame man outside the gate of the temple, begging for alms. Peter told the man, "I have no silver and gold, but I give you what I have; in the name of Jesus Christ of Nazareth, rise and walk" (3:6).

I think of that story very often when I'm out on the streets. I can't make the lame walk or the deaf hear, but I can offer — we *all* can offer — a kind of healing experience by giving what we can: eye contact, a smile, a greeting, or maybe even some extra snacks we have in tow. Sometimes that's all people need, is to be acknowledged, to be recognized, and to receive a sign of welcome, rather than indifference. I've seen lives change because of a simple smile and a touch of the hand. A small act of love, kindness and compassion, an act of mercy, makes the most invisible members of our society truly seen, truly heard through that gift of personal encounter.

What is true of the homeless in Denver is true of homeless everywhere. If you visit the Termini train station in Rome, for example, you will find a large portion of Rome's homeless population hanging out and sleeping there at night, totally unacknowledged by the bustling crowds going in and out.

When Melanie went to Rome, the trip coincided with her birthday. After her birthday dinner, the waiter gave her a box of biscotti to take home. Upon returning to the hotel, she promptly went up to Termini and dispersed the biscotti among the homeless people snuggled up in their sleeping bags or sitting outside the main entrance. One of the women we met was Polish, but she spoke to us in broken Italian, with my friend Elise, the co-author of this book, playing translator. I was so moved because the woman said she liked my dress and thought I was pretty. These people often have such fascinating backgrounds and stories to tell, but they are also among the first victims of what Pope Francis has called a "throwaway culture," where most of us are attached more to money than to human beings.

In Denver, the heart of the action for the homeless happens in two places downtown: Colfax Avenue and the 16th Street Mall. It is difficult to truly understand these places if one hasn't experienced them firsthand, but I'll attempt to paint as clear a picture as possible.

Colfax Avenue, Denver

Colfax Avenue is the longest commercial street in the United States. It first appeared on Denver maps in 1868 as a dirt road, and then became a bustling trolley route in the Mile High City in the 1890s. Along the way it developed a sordid reputation — *Playboy* once referred to Colfax as "the longest, wickedest street in America."

Denver's Cathedral of the Immaculate Conception is on Colfax, with a perfect day and night view of what has become one of the city's biggest drug pipelines. Police continually patrol the area, but the deals still go down; one can witness them anytime, day or night. Even Mass-goers are not infrequently offered a variety of different drugs. Directly across the street is a legal marijuana dispensary, and just down the block, behind a Knights of Columbus Hall, is a needle exchange. At the McDonald's, also across the street from the cathedral, shootings happen at least once a week, if not more. From January to December 2019, Denver County reported a total of 1,166 total crimes involving theft and violence on Colfax Avenue, including 8 murders, 41 rapes, 72 robberies, 181 aggravated assaults, 146 burglaries, 237 larcenies, 266 thefts from vehicles, 213 auto thefts, and 4 instances of arson, according to the Denver Police Department's archives. The bulk of Colorado's violent crime happens in the wider Denver Metropolitan area, and Colfax runs straight through the heart of the city.

One end of Colfax extends all the way to Aurora and has more bars, pubs, restaurants, and motels than you can count. In many of these motels homeless people can find rooms for forty to fifty dollars a night. Police or facilities that assist homeless frequently hand out vouchers that allow people to stay in these motels for a week or more at a time. Often, these people have no money for food or drugs, and that's when trouble starts happening. Many prostitutes and their pimps hang out in these areas in addition to the omnipresent drug dealers. Most of the motels in the area are well kept, but it's obvious from the crowd hanging out on the balconies and on the streets that they are not a friendly space for those who aren't part of the local population. For those who have been accepted by the homeless after gaining their trust, the people on the streets can become friends and even protectors, making sure they don't receive any unwanted advances.

One thing my ministry did in these areas is hand out CoNEHT cards (Colorado Network to End Human Trafficking) to prostitutes and leave them on the desks at the motels. Many of these people, men and women, have been trafficked in from other states or even other countries and are afraid to talk to groups offering assistance. They will, however, take a card and hide it in their underwear. Organizations such as DHM can only hope and pray they will be used.

The other end of Colfax toward Federal Boulevard is in many ways an entirely different story, at least on the surface. The motels on this end tend to be small, dirty, musty, and full of bedbugs. Homeless people, (single or whole families with small children), prostitutes, pimps, and drug users and dealers hang out there. Oftentimes little children, including infants and toddlers, can be found wearing only diapers or underwear playing in the parking lots of the motels. Old chairs, stained couches and blankets, broken toys, and dirty diapers line the entrances to the rooms. Bugs, rats, mice, cats, and dogs play alongside the children. There is usually a smell wafting from the doorways that would be enough to make anyone run if they weren't called to this ministry.

But people can make a difference, even in places like this. Just a bottle of water or a pair of gloves on a cold night is like giving someone a gold brick. The people who live in these places are so thankful for any assistance they get. Once the mothers know you are only trying to help, they will sit on the curb telling you stories about their kids. You can see these happy little moments and the harsh reality of their daily lives juxtaposed with the life they dream their family may one day live. They will tell you of their hopes that something big is going to happen that will change everything. Though in your heart you know only a miracle would change their circumstances, you keep praying that they don't lose hope until something good actually happens.

The 16th Street Mall, Denver

The 16th Street Mall itself runs only one and a quarter miles long, and extends down 16th Street in downtown Denver, stretching from Broadway Street to Wewatta Street at Union Station. A free mall shuttle runs from one end to the other, with rides beginning at 5:00 a.m. on weekdays and 5:30 a.m. on weekends, and ending just before midnight. The sidewalks and streets were designed by Chinese American architect Ieoh Ming to resemble a western diamondback rattlesnake's scale pattern. This seems to be a metaphor for the area, particularly in terms of how homeless people are treated and how they fight back. If you are visiting, there are many outside places to sit, rest, talk, and eat; but if you are home-less, or appear to be homeless, you will be asked to move along or possibly be fined. These fines add up and failure to pay them or go to court will result in jail time and probation.

Walking past Wewatta Street, you will reach the light rail, which takes you to and from the Denver International Airport and to many of Denver's suburbs. Next to the light rail you can walk up the stairs situated between high rises or take the eleva-tor (if it's working) to the top, overlooking the tracks and a park. Walking down the stairs, past coffee shops, bars, and restaurants, you will reach the park, which has a hill in the middle and is near the Platte River. This is Commons Park, better known among street kids as "Stoner Hill." This is where most homeless spend their time: on Stoner Hill or along the Platte, although police and neighborhood leaders are currently lobbying to change this in a concerted effort to control transients and illegal drug activity.

On any given day or night, you could find "kids" ranging in age from nine to twenty-five hanging out, sleeping, or doing drugs on the Hill. The area along the Platte is infested with large black rats. Most homeless have become so used to living with them that they just kick them out of the way when they become a nuisance.

In the same area are bridges where many people sleep at night. The bridges have concrete pillars sectioning off spaces that people will stake out as their own "cubby" for the night or for as long as they can keep others out, including the police. It's not the safest or coziest place to call home. There are also many tunnels along the Platte where drug addicts hole up and take shelter. Plywood is frequently placed over the stream of water flowing down the center of the tunnels and mattresses are placed on top for makeshift beds. At times, whole families — mother and father and children — will sleep there until they find or qualify for housing.

There is another such tunnel, under a place called Skate Park, that my organization used for training purposes when volunteers first signed up to help with our evening ministry, "Street-Beetz." As part of the training, newbies were taken as far back in the tunnel as is safe, not necessarily from homeless, but other varmints living underground. This tunnel is filled with graffiti, sleeping bags, clothes, and food sitting on little ledges. Many homeless who are there during trainings do not cause trouble but invite the group to continue on their way. During the training, volunteers carry spray paint so they can leave messages of hope on top of the graffiti. Most messages are painted over multiple times, but some are still visible, even after six or seven years. When the group is done spray-painting, they turn off their cell phone flashlights and slowly make their way back out of the tunnel until they see the small dot of light start to get bigger. When asked how seeing the light made them feel, most respond, "relieved" and "unafraid" as they knew there was a way out.

And that right there is the point of my ministry's approach that I have tried to implement: Those who work with the ministry are to be that "light at the end of the tunnel" for the homeless people they meet, to show them there is a way out of that life if they want it — and, eventually, they can point people to the True Light, Jesus, with their love and actions.

Beyond the other side of the 16th Street Mall is a place called Civic Center Park near Denver's capitol building and the Golden Triangle, which is bordered by Colfax Avenue, North Broadway Boulevard, and Speer Boulevard. This is where a group of homeless known on the streets as the *juggalos* typically hang out. In general, this community distinguishes itself from the homeless crowd called the *gutter punks* — the crowd that spends their time near the 16th Street Mall and the Denver Rescue Mission on Broadway. The main difference between the two groups is essentially gang ties; however, there is also a bit of a cultural difference. The gutter punks tend to be younger, more tied to gangs, and in search of an alternative way of living. They are also generally seen as more unruly and prone to cause problems, rejecting norms and trying to carve out places for themselves like Stoner Hill.

There are so many things that happen on "the Hill," under the bridges, and in the tunnels: beatings, murders, rapes, and suicides, just to name a few. There are two stories here that I think perfectly reflect both the challenges that homeless face, and the unexpected generosity they can find.

The first is about a man who lived under a viaduct that had several concrete pillars, which he made into different "rooms." In his first concrete enclosure, he had hauled in items from alleys and dumpsters, forming a makeshift kitchen with a stove that didn't work, but could function as a fire pit. He also put in a small refrigerator that held coolers, a table and chairs, shelving, cookware, dishes, glasses, and silverware. The next "cubby" resembled a living room or office area, with a sofa, chair, and desk. The last "cubby" was his bedroom, fully furnished with a bedroom ensemble including bedside tables and lanterns. Across the front of the man's living space hung big blue tarps for privacy. Then one day the police came. What they couldn't haul away, they burned. This happens in Denver so often it's enough to bring tears to anyone who sees the hurt and hopelessness of people who were just trying to survive.

The other story involves REI, a large outdoor store in downtown Denver, directly on the Platte River. One day a homeless man was sleeping close to the Platte River under a walkway, and a manager from REI came out to talk to him. The man, expecting to have the police called on him, immediately jumped up and apologized for sleeping there. (Denver has a "no right to rest" policy, meaning that if you are caught sleeping or sitting for too long, you could be fined or arrested. Homeless who can't pay these fines often end up in jail.) As the man was getting ready to run away, as he usually does, the store manager told him to hold on for a minute, and told him that "you can't sleep here like this." The man, sure the police wouldn't be far behind, kept apologizing to the manager, but he was told he needed to come up into the store, and together they found him the items he needed to be more comfortable under the walkway. The manager ended up giving the man a sleeping bag, jacket, gloves, a lantern, and packets of freeze-dried camping food. This is another story which, for those who know homelessness, is also enough to cause tears, but ones that warm the heart.

The people featured in this book have all experienced some or all of these things to varying degrees. Their stories include drug and alcohol abuse, sexual assault, trauma, mental disorders, and theft. They tell of broken hearts and broken lives, hardened by years of bitterness, self-protection, and feeling lower than the scum of the earth. But these stories also tell, each in its own way, how one person can change all that simply by looking beyond the hardened shells of self-defense and embracing the vulnerable, insecure soul longing to be loved that lies underneath; how one person who points to them and calls them by name — like Jesus to Matthew the tax collector in Caravaggio's masterful depiction of that moment in *The Calling of Matthew* — can help them sift through the broken pieces of their lives and rediscover hope, dignity, and the desire to strive for something better.

Being Human in a "Throwaway Culture"

In an interview with papal biographer Austen Ivereigh, published in April 2020, Pope Francis lamented certain social distancing mechanisms for homeless taken during the COVID-19 outbreak, saying, "A photo appeared the other day of a parking lot in Las Vegas where they had been put in quarantine. And the hotels were empty. But the homeless cannot go to a hotel. That is the throwaway culture in practice."*

This was spot on, because most hotels won't just let home-less people sleep there for free, even during a pandemic; yet the homeless cannot afford to stay in even a cheap hotel, at least not for more than a night or two.

Thankfully, there are some exceptions. In March 2020, I had one Denver hotel owner contact me during the lockdown to ask if I knew of someone who needed a place to stay for a nominal fee. I passed her the information to different ministries working with the homeless, so grateful for this tangible act of compassion and mercy.

Since he was elected in 2013, Pope Francis has made a point of prioritizing those on the margins of society, including mi-grants, the homeless, and those in prison, often stressing that no one is beyond God's reach, no one is beyond his mercy and for-giveness. During his homily at a penitential liturgy in St. Peter's Basilica in March 2015, Pope Francis told attendees that God will pardon our every sin if we turn to him: "He really is 'rich in mercy' and extends His mercy with abundance over those who turn to Him with a sincere heart. ... No one can be excluded from the mercy of God; everyone knows the way to access it and the Church is the house that welcomes all and refuses no one."†

This is certainly a beautiful thought from the Holy Father, but how many times have we put it into action? How many homeless people feel welcomed by our local churches? How many were left exposed, out in the open, as the rest of us remained safely at home when COVID hit?

How many times a day might we ourselves walk right by those who need our compassion, love, and hugs? Many of these

*As quoted in "Pope: How I am Living through the Covid-19 Pandemic," Vatican News, April 8, 2020, https://www.vaticannews.va/en/pope/news/2020-04/pope-how-i-am-living-through-the -covid-19-pandemic.html.

†As quoted in "Pope Francis: Homily with Announcement of Year of Mercy," *America*, March 16, 2015, https://www.americamagazine.org/issue/pope-francis-homily-announcement-year-mercy.

people might not even be homeless but are simply in need of some gesture that says, "I believe in you," or, "You are worth so much more than you realize." For the homeless, this need is often more fundamental than food, shelter, and hygiene. And these gestures can be so easily made if we are able to look outside our own personal wants, needs, and desires, and into the lives and hearts of others.

Rising from Rock Bottom

For ten years, Denver Homeless Ministry in Denver, worked with the homeless population of our area, helping them to lift themselves up and to remind them that there is a loving God who is interested and involved in their lives. In addition, for eight years we organized and led annual private pilgrimages to Rome for homeless youth and a few older adults as a means of inspiring them to change their lives and not to allow themselves to be controlled by their circumstances.

As you'll read later in this book, my story is not unlike that of many of those living on the streets today: It's a story full of pain, trauma, and recovery. And yet God has raised me up and allowed me to use those painful experiences to help others, something I am so grateful for. Like them, I am a work in progress. And so, I asked my friend, Elise Ann Allen — who is a journalist in Rome with the *Crux* news site, and who has met every single person in this book — to help me share not only some of the memorable encounters that I've experienced in over a decade of ministry, but how those encounters affected me personally, and have helped me learn more about the merciful heart of God.

I first met Elise in Denver around 2011. At the time, she was discerning religious life and had joined a group of volunteers who came with us on our outreach nights. Like everyone else who wants to volunteer with my ministry, she went through the training I require and came out with us regularly until she moved to Rome as a Vatican correspondent in 2013, just a few months before I began thinking about the Rome pilgrimages. Since then, Elise has reported on every single trip we've taken, and has interviewed nearly every person who came, many of whom she already knew from her time working with DHM in Denver.

Elise also helped arrange up-front tickets at papal audiences for several of the homeless so they could meet the pope, and after she got married in 2020, she and her husband John had our group over to their home for dinner that year, where John prepared a traditional Italian meal and made the girls who came feel like VIPs! So, when it came time to choose a co-author for this book — because I write like I talk, in total disarray! — Elise was a natural fit. In fact, she told me during the writing process that she actually heard my voice in her head when she was working on it, so if that doesn't tell you the kind of relationship we have and her closeness to these people, I don't know what does!

My hope in telling these stories is that they will touch and inspire you as much as they have me. I hope that by getting a window into their lives, you will be reminded of God's providence, and be persuaded that there is a loving God who is interested and involved in each of our lives; that you will catch a glimpse of the humanity of these people, and of the God who shows his love for us by listening, caring for, and remaining with us on every step of our journey, even if we can't always see it.

I hope, perhaps most fundamentally, that these stories will rip open the doors of people's hearts and challenge them to go outside of their comfort zones, ushering in a deeper, more exhilarating love that does not look past the people they encounter, that does not tilt the head in the opposite direction when they see someone in need like Jesus who, upon the blind man Bartimaeus's plea, "Jesus, Son of David, have mercy on me!" stops and asks, "What do you want me to do for you?" (see Lk 18:38, 41).

I hope that these stories will tear down the barriers that so often keep us anesthetized and indifferent to the lives and needs of others. I hope that they will lead to a true *metanoia* resulting in a more compassionate and merciful approach to all people, but especially those we might otherwise be most disposed to dismiss.

The people featured in this book have all experienced the helplessness of Bartimaeus to varying degrees — the feeling of being at the mercy of a system they are powerless to change for themselves.

This book recounts how our ministry, the Denver Homeless Ministry, played a role in helping these eight individuals who used to live on and off the streets to take serious steps toward changing their lives through a unique approach focused on respect, love, and friendship. The "culture of encounter" Pope Francis so often advocates as a remedy to the throwaway culture might at times seem ambiguous and out of grasp, but these stories show the culture of encounter in action. They make evident how going out to meet people where they are, and lending them a helping hand rather than looking past them, how looking at someone and loving them in the same way Jesus looked at the rich young man in Scripture, can change the course of a life and spread a little more good in the world.

Through my own experience of healing, which culminated in my conversion to the Catholic Church, I have been able to play a cherished role in helping each of these people to see their own worth and to view themselves not as the world does, but as God does. The Rome pilgrimages have been a key part of this, allowing these people to experience not only the beauty of an important ancient culture, but the deep spiritual heritage of Italy through meeting the pope, and visits to the breathtaking churches and monuments that line the streets of the Eternal City.

One thing that every person said at some point during the trip is that for them, going was proof that "good things can happen," and that life wasn't all sadness and pain. In each case, regardless of their faith, these people have come back changed in some way, and that in itself is perhaps the openness that Jesus seeks when he knocks at the doors of our hearts. In reading these stories, I hope that your heart will also be changed.

1

TANYA

We Find Ourselves in Helping Others

How I viewed other people didn't start to change until I encountered St. John Paul II's theology of the body at a parish study group in Boulder, Colorado. I began seeing others for who they were, not for what they were going to do for me — or to me. Acquiring this perspective, of course, took time and grace, but my hunger for this new way of thinking and living kept me moving forward. Love also took on new meaning. I wanted to love and be loved, but before I could love others rightly, I had to first learn to love God. I still saw him as one who loved us only if we did things exactly right.

Losing Innocence

As an adolescent, and for much of my early adult life, I was beyond lost. I grew up in Rock Island, Illinois, in a housing project named the Manor Courts, three hours west of Chicago, where poor white people lived. A few blocks away were the Arsenal Courts, where poor black people lived. For us kids who grew up in the projects, we did everything that our imaginations could conjure up. Our behavior seemed "normal," because everyone around us was doing the same thing — it's just that the only norm we knew was what we saw on television. Even though deep down I knew that the Hollywood lifestyle was false, I wanted to have that lifestyle, but because I could never attain what I saw, I became depressed. TV makes sex and drugs seem glamorous, but once caught in that trap you realize it's all a lie. I always felt I had to prove myself to the other kids. In brief, I lived a depraved life, one filled with illicit sex, drugs, alcohol, and an endless effort to be worthy. Today, I take great comfort in the teachings of Pope John Paul II, who said that even in these distorted pursuits, we are all actually searching for the good. In our desire for "union and communion" we often settle for counterfeits, and I was no exception.

My paternal grandparents were originally from Bulgaria but fled to the United States after my grandfather killed a man in a bar fight. They raised my father and my aunt in America, but their Bulgarian roots still ran deep. In Bulgaria, family loyalty is a great virtue, even if one of the family members is a bad egg. It was this sense of loyalty, I believe, which later caused my grandparents to protect their son, my father, despite his repeated physical and verbal abuse of my mother, my sister, and me.

My childhood and early teen years can be described as

horrific. By the time I was three, feuding between my parents had escalated to the point that my mother finally had enough after being beaten nearly to death on the side of the road. She divorced my father and managed to secure a job and a small apartment for us, no small feat for a single mother in the 1950s. My paternal grandparents would babysit me from time to time. At one point, my grandparents told me my mother had died, and they put me in an orphanage in hopes my mother would forget about me and they would be able to legally adopt me. When I tried to tell the orphanage directors of my plight, they didn't believe me, so I stopped eating. After six weeks, I was admitted to the hospital for malnutrition and only then were the police made aware of my situation and able to locate my mother. I was returned to her and my little sister Maria, and I was relieved to know that my mother was actually alive, as I had always thought! But little did I know that was not going to be the most traumatic part of my childhood.

The years that followed were filled with constant fleeing from my father and grandparents. We eventually left Illinois for Georgia, where a great-uncle offered us his help with babysitting and paying the bills. We jumped at his offer of kindness — but his offer had nothing to do with compassion.

From the ages of three to six, this man molested me and allowed others to do the same. I suffered unspeakable violations in my own home and in his remote mountain house. I already had suspicions about men because of my father, but this experience solidified those beyond repair, or so I thought at the time. By the time I was ten, I had tried to take my life several times, and I was engaged in the now-common phenomenon known as cutting. I was warned never to speak of the abuse to my mother, so I started to make threats when the abuse happened. Seeking to protect my younger sister, I began to have a certain sense of power over the abusers, threatening them to stay away from her lest I reveal their crimes. I vividly recall one instance when my great-uncle slapped my sister over and over, causing her to bleed from the mouth, because she would not eat a fried egg sandwich he had made. My threat of telling my mother worked, because he stopped, and I continued to keep quiet.

It was because of these experiences that I came to believe at a very young age, perhaps as young as six, that sex was equivalent to power. Although I may not have understood it in those terms, the association was embedding itself in my already-warped psyche. By allowing the abuse to happen, I could control certain situations. I could stop a grown man from abusing my younger sister, or secure an abundance of candy and even money from him. In these young years, I even began to understand survival skills, hiding the accumulated candy and cash and saving it for when I would need to buy loyalty or some other short-term solution, even with other kids in the neighborhood.

My abuse finally ended one day when my mother overheard me telling my uncle that if he didn't give me what I wanted, I was going to tell her what he was doing. That night she chased him out of the house with a butcher knife. Yet instead of feeling relief, in my distorted sense of love I felt sadness, as I thought that this man who had abused me loved me and I didn't want him to go. When I was brought to the hospital to be examined, the doctor said I had been raped repeatedly, perhaps since the age of three, and that to talk about it would traumatize me further. This was 1957. I was thirty-four before my mother and I had a heart-to-heart about what happened. She had no idea that I remembered everything. She told me through tears that if she had "done things differently, not listened to the doctors, my life would have been so much better." I told her, my life of love and forgiveness had a whole new meaning. I didn't regret all I went through, because many people have learned to love and forgive because I did.

After the falling out with my uncle, who cleaned out the joint bank account, we were broke and were forced to move back to Illinois into the old apartment we had been living in — meaning we again had to endure harassment from my father. Any time he came near the projects, someone warned my mother that he was in town and was packing a gun. On one occasion, my mother decided to confront him. My sister and I were to hide in the apartment. When she approached his car, she saw a gun lying on the passenger seat. He said he had come for me, and she told him to shoot her and get it over with. When he drove away, my mother turned to leave and saw several retired army guys standing behind her, and she knew they had her back. That story was told over and over again in the projects. I felt so proud.

I finally met my father again several years later, spending a week with him after I graduated from high school. The meeting was difficult and awkward. I didn't trust my father, and it was evident to me at the time that he didn't value me too much: I was assigned to sleep in a tiny room on a cot. I ended up calling my sister to come and get me. I simply couldn't stay in his roach- and mouse-infested hovel. Yet, I have since come to believe that he did really love me, in the only way he knew how.

Lacking the Look of Love

Through all these experiences I learned how to be a survivor, to trust no one, and to seek out friends I could boss around, use, manipulate, and terrorize in my desire to get what I wanted. I learned to steal, and I began to use sex to manipulate people and situations. I taught other children how to shoplift and would then take their stolen goods to the pawn shop. Many years later I met one of my thieving disciples, who by then had spent time in reform school because of her stealing habits. To this day, I pray for her and repent of having led her astray.

By the time I was twenty, I was unhappy, depressed, and

extremely overweight. My obesity only made my thirst for love worse, as I had a lot of friends but none of them seemed interested in dating me. Desiring intimacy in any way that I could get it, I made myself available for sex. During tough financial times, I would request money in exchange for sex, even though I would have denied that this essentially made me a prostitute. Too many times, I ended up in the back seat of a car or truck, a restroom, or an alley — to make money, but also to satisfy my need for love in a very misconstrued way. At this time, I was also regularly using potent drugs and indulging in cheap liquor. Life was good, or so I thought. But the truth is, by that time I had seen so many divorces, suicides, abortions, acts of self-mutilation, and overall depravity that I just wanted to leave this world. One night I ingested twelve bottles of various over-the-counter pills and ended up in the hospital for nearly two weeks. The shock was waking up to realize I was still alive!

Many years later, I heard the story of St. Nonnus of Edessa and Saint Pelagia. It is one that pierces the heart of any woman who has been used and abused, but it also offers extraordinary hope for anyone who has been sexually wounded or who has wounded another.

Saint Nonnus was a fifth-century Catholic bishop who, through the grace of God, had come to understand deeply the plight of humanity. He saw that, despite the degradation all around him, God was the author of human life and that human life was therefore beautiful. He must have also had a particular insight into the pains of women, because one day, Bishop Nonnus was walking with another cleric when both saw a beautiful woman — likely a prostitute — walking toward them. Not wanting to lust after this alluring woman, the companion of Bishop Nonnus turned his eyes away as she passed. After she had gone by, the companion saw that Bishop Nonnus had tears in his eyes. He also realized that the bishop had not turned his gaze away from the woman as she went by but had looked right at her. A bit baffled and concerned, he asked, "Brother bishop, why did you not turn away from this woman?" Nonnus replied, "What a tragedy it is that such beauty would be sold to the lust of men." The woman obviously noticed the bishop's stare too because she later sought him out. Prompted by the loving response of the saintly bishop, she experienced a conversion to Christianity. Despite her life choices, she experienced a piercing love in Nonnus's simple, chaste look into both her eyes and soul. We now know her as Saint Pelagia.

I'd never experienced this kind of look myself until I met Fr. Michael O'Loughlin, a man who would become my father in faith. He was the pastor of the parish I would eventually make my home. If you had told me even a few years before that a man could look on me with love without wanting something more, I would have laughed and let out a surly, "Yeah, right!" But this look of love would still be a long time coming, though I see now that God's timing was perfect.

A New Journey Begins

After my overdose, I knew I was a mess, so I agreed to a friend's request to speak with the Lutheran pastor of someone she knew. I'm sure it shocked many of his parishioners when I pulled up to Holy Cross Lutheran Church on my motorcycle. But the pastor received me kindly and began talking to me about Christianity. As a dizzy twenty-six-year-old, I heard little more than a monotonous babble of "church talk." At one point he asked me, "If you were to die tonight, do you know for sure you would go to heaven?" He seemed taken aback when I replied, "I couldn't care less."

He then invited me to participate in a Bible study and, against my strongest inclinations, I agreed because a good friend of mine had urged me to. Never had anyone set something up for me and invited others to join so I wouldn't feel self-conscious. I felt slightly overwhelmed and yet honored. I attended the Bible study for several months and then was invited to join another Bible study made up of young adults, an invitation I finally accepted after declining many times. Despite my initial impressions that this large group of people was a bunch of "goody-goodies," I had a change of heart after experiencing their genuine faith and goodness. Later that night, I asked Jesus to help me know him, and I made a commitment to live for him.

Over the next few months, I got to know the couple who led the Bible study, Otis and DeAnne Anderson. They invited me to stay with them until I got back on my feet, and my decision to say yes is likely the most pivotal decision I ever made. Although it did not happen overnight, God turned my life around. I changed my appearance, stopped using profanity, and softened my heart toward God and others. The Andersons put up with a lot and being loved so openly was a challenge for me. I was a bit like an animal that, after being beaten for many years, cowers with fear when its new owner simply goes to pat it on the head.

I eventually left the Andersons's home to attend an evangelical Christian discipleship training school in Texas. The discipleship training school was run by David Wilkerson, author of the Christian classic *The Cross and the Switchblade*. Brother Dave, as we called him, was as gracious as a host could be. In time, he and his wife, Gwen, invited me to live with their family and to serve as Gwen's companion as she was living through her first bout of cancer and treatments. After three months or so, leaders from the Mark IV Christian Youth Ministry invited me to join them in their ministry as they moved to Mississippi. Brother Dave, however, strongly counseled against the move, as he had come to believe that the group was cult-like, and he offered to help me find another ministry. At the time, I didn't accept his negative view of Mark IV and decided to travel with the group to Mississippi, but I soon discovered that Brother Dave was right. We were engaged in constant evangelism, we traveled only in groups of two, I wasn't allowed any contact with family or friends, and I was also harshly chastised for breaking the rules.

I eventually left Mark IV and went back to the Andersons, who assisted me in attending the local junior college and in trying to repair my relationship with my family. Later, I enrolled at Concordia University in suburban Chicago in the fall of 1980. During this time, I was still overweight and developed anorexia. I spent twelve weeks in the hospital overcoming my eating disorder, but little did I realize that it was my inward image that needed reconstructive surgery. The one great consolation from this period is that I graduated from Concordia with a major in sociology and a minor in theology.

Soon after this I met a man — whom I'll call "Robert" — at a bar owned by Chicago Bear Walter Payton. It was minutes before midnight on New Year's Eve 1985. I don't know whether it was the euphoria of the pre-midnight moment or my low self-esteem, but we hit it off instantly. Four days later, we were engaged; two weeks later, we were living together. Robert was Catholic, so I started attending church with him shortly after we started living together. Somehow, I didn't see any conflict between my Christian faith and engaging in premarital sex, but I believed that if we were going to be married, we needed to attend the same church. Eight months later, we were married in the Catholic Church, even though I was not Catholic.

Our marriage lasted nearly twenty years before we were eventually divorced. On one level I suppose that's impressive, but our relationship was seriously dysfunctional from the very beginning. Robert viewed me as inferior and, as a result, he was demanding and controlling. Hard as I tried, I could never live up to his standards or please him. I also continued to struggle with bulimia throughout our marriage, yet Robert continually denied my request for counseling. I believe the only truly blessed thing from that time was that it planted the roots for my eventual conversion to the Catholic Church.

During the early years of our marriage, I was a "double dipper" when it came to church attendance. On Saturday night we would attend the local Catholic parish, and on Sundays I would attend a well-known mega-church in the Chicago area. When I traveled, I would attend various Protestant churches; I couldn't bring myself to engage in "Catholic stuff" when I wasn't with Robert. In fact, during my trips to other churches, I would spend a fair amount of time trying to get Catholics to become Protestant. Even in our Catholic parish, I used the forum of the Bible study to make the participants question their allegiance to the Church. Attending Mass was a bit of a ruse for spousal unity rather than real belief.

Robert and I moved to Colorado in 1996 so that he could attend law school, after leaving medical school and working in car dealerships as a consultant. We searched out several Catholic churches and finally settled on St. Thomas Aquinas Parish in Boulder. After being at the parish for about seven years, I heard a homily by the associate pastor, Fr. David Dwyer, now director of the popular radio show *Busted Halo*, in which he used the phrase, "Catholic Christian." I later emailed him, stating that this phrase was an oxymoron because "everyone knows that Catholics aren't really Christians." He sent me a lengthy reply that was filled with verses from the Bible explaining and defending Catholic teaching. I was blown away; I didn't think a Catholic priest could quote Scripture so skillfully. Not long after, we met, and he corrected my misconceptions about the Catholic Church and its teachings. I was embarrassed at how closed to the Church my mind had been for so many years.

In 2003, I was received into the Catholic Church and accepted all the Church's teachings, except certain moral issues which I would wrestle with for a few more years. I was confirmed by

Archbishop Charles Chaput of Denver, now the retired Archbishop of Philadelphia, and Father Dave was my sponsor.

Finding Healing

I was first introduced to St. John Paul II's theology of the body at a study group through my parish, and although I initially resisted it, I became intrigued. The program is a series of lectures given by John Paul II during his weekly Wednesday general audiences between September 5, 1979, and November 28, 1984, offering an analysis on human sexuality. Those speeches were eventually consolidated into an instructive program on Church's teaching about sex and human sexuality. There has been some debate about it among Catholic theologians, but I had no clue about any of that, and it came into my life and helped me enormously at a very pivotal time.

Since I had such a poor image of myself, I struggled greatly with the idea that "the body is very good." Because of my sordid sexual past, I had difficulty with the lofty ideas that sex is beautiful and that a man could actually avoid lusting after a woman. Yet when I discovered the theology of the body, I learned that God's love is unconditional. Once this reality set in, I could begin to believe that others — my family, my friends, my pastor — could have the same kind of love. I marveled when I first heard the quote about God's nature from the *Catechism*, "God has revealed his innermost secret: God himself is an eternal exchange of love, Father, Son and Holy Spirit, and he has destined us to share in that exchange."* Imagine that! We are called to participate in the very inner life of God!

I began to ask myself, if I really believe all that I have come to learn, what do I do with it? How do I, the woman with a sordid past who has regained her own dignity, help others to do the

---

*Catechism of the Catholic Church, 2nd ed (Washington, DC: Libreria Editrice Vaticana–United States Conference of Catholic Bishops, 2000), 221.

same? I prayed, "Lord, teach me your ways, direct my path, may every fiber of my being unite in reference to your name." Like Moses asked the Lord to send Aaron to preach to Pharaoh in his place, I did not feel smart enough or worthy enough and was willing to help someone else do his will. Yet my desire for an easy path was not what the Lord was asking of me.

Founding a Ministry

Once dignity is restored in a wounded life, that life is changed forever, as my own personal story has revealed. And once mercy is received and acknowledged, it must be lived out. Since founding the Denver Homeless Ministry, I've found over the years that many of the stories I hear on the streets mimic my own past. I never set out to establish a homeless ministry, and how it even came about was a total accident.

As I said earlier, after Robert and I divorced, I moved from Boulder to Denver, and close to the Capitol building, where I would often go to eat dinner, sitting on the steps and reading a book, since I didn't really have many friends yet. When that first woman approached me and started talking to me about simple stuff as if we were already friends, I started to feel like I had finally had the fellowship I was craving. As time passed by more people joined us. Then one day one of my new friends asked if anyone had anything to eat because her appointment went so long that she missed the last "feed" for the evening. None of us had anything, so she said she was heading to the 16th Street Mall to *spange* (ask for spare change) or ask for "white boxes" (people's leftovers). That was the first time I realized my new friends were homeless. I was amazed at how comfortable I felt and how accepted I was. The next night I brought some sandwiches, and everyone loved them and asked what shelter I had gotten them from!

When the weather started changing, they invited me to their

shelter next to the courthouse, where they sat on a grate with blankets and sleeping bags. The heat would keep us very warm, and a tarp over the top kept everyone dry. After this encounter, I started asking people at work for socks, food, toiletries — anything I thought might help make my friends' lives a little easier as they lay down on the heated grate at night to sleep.

Soon people would ask if they could join me in my homeless ministry. I would answer, "What homeless ministry? These people are my friends." One day a young seminarian, Mason Farley (now Father Mason), asked me if I would lead him and another seminarian friend on a homeless walk through the park. We met a gentleman who called himself King David. King David gave me a silver ring to try on. Laughingly I put it on my middle finger on my left hand, so he said, "Now we're married." I reminded him it was the wrong finger, and I tried to take it off. Yet all these years later, the ring still won't budge. It has remained on my finger to remind me always to let the Lord lead! This was the beginning of many "homeless walks" I would do over a course of twelve years.

I almost gave up homeless ministry altogether when I met a young girl called Lucinda, who was known as "Binky" on the streets. She got her name from picking up a pacifier on the ground and putting it in her mouth. The street kids named her Binky, and it stuck. She was fifteen and one of the nicest, sweetest, shyest kids I had met on the streets. It took some months before she would talk to me and become my friend. You could tell there was a lot going on in both her mind and body. The kids on the street took her in, watched after her, made her feel cared for and loved. Finally, I and several different Denver street ministers convinced her that she was worth so much more and she needed to get into a shelter and finish high school. She simply needed to be cared for, and she finally agreed — but because she was only fifteen, she had to wait for her sixteenth birthday to enter a shelter, as none would take kids at that age at that time (the age has since been lowered). The waiting was hard, but we kept trying to encourage her as she only had two weeks to wait. But the night before she was ready to go, her boyfriend was arrested and put in jail, so she went into her closet and hung herself. For those who believe they have no hope, losing what might seem like the last glimmer of it is the saddest thing one can experience. I saw myself in this young lady; I saw so much hope, I saw a future for her that she didn't see for herself, and I was absolutely heartbroken. (Little did I know, just ten years later Binky's little sister Angelique would be one of the people I brought to Rome.)

On the way home from Binky's funeral, I called my spiritual director and pastor, Fr. Michael O'Loughlin, to tell him that I was done with homeless ministry. I simply couldn't do it anymore. He told me that might be true, but that I needed to pray about it, and that if the Lord wanted me to continue, he would strengthen me; if he had another plan for my life, he would show me the way. My fear was that my heart would be hardened, that death on the streets would no longer hurt and would become just a part of daily life. I prayed hard about whether to continue, and in the end I did. Soon after, the Denver Homeless Ministry began.

As most of us know, so often only hindsight often permits us to see the whys of our questions. I understood what Binky went through because of my past. Coming to terms with your past doesn't take away the hurt you feel for others; it allows you not to be stagnant. It gives you courage to stand strong and reach out. Survival doesn't have to be negative. In our desire for "union and communion," in our desire to "love and be loved," Pope John Paul says we often settle for counterfeits, but in time we can learn to believe that there is a God who does love us.

Often people who don't know me or know my past ask me why I do what I do, going out on the streets in the pouring rain, freezing cold, or knee-deep snow when, maybe, only one life was touched. In these moments, I remember the words of Mother

Teresa, who said: "Never worry about numbers. Help one person at a time and always start with the person nearest you."

One of my favorite stories involves meeting a man in his thirties on the 16th Street Mall in Denver, where we were handing out items for youth. We served twenty-five-and-under youth mostly at that time, yet never turned someone in need away. This man approached me on one of the coldest February nights I ever experienced in Denver, seventeen degrees below zero. He said he just wanted to talk to someone. He told me how he wanted to be an artist but was an alcoholic and his mother-in-law had had enough and kicked him out and he could not come back and stay with his wife and child until he "cleaned up his act."

He said he was living in a tent under the bridge. I stayed and listened to his story. To be honest, I was freezing, and I just wanted to go home. I finally offered him a bottle of water. He kept talking and I kept getting colder. I found myself praying silently to the Lord that his tongue would freeze to the top of his mouth so he would stop talking, yet I could see and feel his hurt. He needed to know that I saw him, that he wasn't invisible, but that he was a real person with a real need. Finally, I told him it was time for me to leave, and I took off my gloves and gave them to him since I was going home, and I thought he needed them more than me. I thought that would be the end of it and I'd never see him again. That's generally how it is on the streets.

About six months later I was meeting up with a friend on the mall when I stopped to watch a man paint amazing pictures with spray paint. There was a crowd of about twenty-five people standing around watching, waiting for him to finish the last part of his painting. Before he did that, he stopped and said,

I'm going to finish this in a moment, but I want to tell you a story. My life was not always this good. One day I had hit rock bottom and I didn't think that I could make it anymore. Then I met a woman that simply listened to me and looked me in the eyes as I talked. She seemed to believe in me. She gave me a bottle of water, took off her own gloves to give to me and gave me a hug before leaving. I went back to my tent under the bridge and said to myself, "If a complete stranger can believe in me, then I need to change and start believing in myself." I quit drinking, I went back to my family, and this is my wife and daughter whom I would like to introduce to the woman who changed my life.

He pointed to me through the crowd and asked, "Do you remember me?" I did then, even though I hadn't recognized him at first, as everything about him had changed! As the crowd turned to look, I had tears in my eyes as I thanked the Lord again and again for allowing me to see the fruits of my ministry.

All Roads Lead to Rome

Around ten years ago, I had a very powerful dream about taking a homeless person from the streets of Denver to Rome. I woke up thinking, this surely can't be from the Lord — I don't have the marketing skills, the connections, or the money to take on a project this big. So I had a little talk with the Lord. I told him yes, but I wanted to make sure he understood that I would only do this if I was sure it came from him. After dreaming about this for six months, he finally laid someone on my heart and the process began. It hasn't been easy, but it has been totally amazing. Every single life involved has changed, including my own.

In Rome, I saw many of the people I took blossom. There were many difficult experiences, and some truly awful moments that I would not want to live through again, but there was also a lot of good. I saw many of these people open up in ways that neither they nor I really expected. It's funny how just taking them outside of their daily routine and comfort zone can reveal sides I had never seen — the seemingly hardened and standoffish became sweet, even meek, and the noisy and outgoing became quiet and contemplative. If you ask the homeless who made the trip, some of their favorite moments were not visiting museums and ancient monuments, as much as they loved those, but serving the homeless in Rome. A man whose street name was "Tree" said for years after the Rome trip that his favorite time was when we spent a morning working with the Missionaries of Charity in their soup kitchen right next to the Vatican, doing dishes, prepping food, and cleaning up. He also enjoyed handing out spare coins to gypsy women begging around the city — even though a big motive for this was to flirt with them, there was something genuine about his charity.

Most people either don't know or don't realize that the homeless can be the most loving and giving people you'll ever find. You see, when the homeless set out to give away their leftovers, like they do in Rome, it's normal to them. For me, oftentimes I'm torn — do I have another great meal, or do I give it away? Giving it away always wins out, yet the thought of keeping it for myself crosses my mind and heart first. I believe the homeless people I've met should all be saints. It's not that they are perfect, but in their own way, they have taught me unconditional love.

Mother Teresa once said, "I see Jesus in every human being ... I say to myself; this is hungry Jesus, I must feed him. This is sick Jesus. This one has leprosy or gangrene; I must wash him and tend to him. I serve because I love Jesus." For Mother Teresa, it was Jesus who inspired her to serve, as it should be for each of us. I wish I were as wholesome and loving as she was, but I see so many faults and hurts that, at times, I feel tainted. Yet in spite of this, I know Jesus uses me through my soiled and sinful journey, and to me, that is the reason to serve and love all of his people. He has given me a love I didn't believe was possible, a love for those who feel unloved, useless, and invisible. When I help others in even the smallest of ways, I do not find myself, I find Jesus. He becomes real.

My homeless friends bring Jesus to life!

2

CLARISSA

We Long to See and Be Seen

Saint Augustine once said that "the deepest desire of the human heart is to see another and be seen by that other."* While this is probably the case for everyone, it rings especially true for the homeless, who often feel like they're invisible, especially to those around them who live in the same cities or neighborhoods. So often, their deepest desire is to be seen for who they are and who they can be, not for the circumstances they're in.

One of the greatest joys of my life has been getting to know each of my homeless friends. They all have this hard outer shell,

---

*See St. Augustine of Hippo, *Sermon* 69, 2 and 3.

but underneath it, there are real flesh-and-blood people who have soft hearts and big dreams for what they want their lives to be. Getting to see that is special, and inspiring. And the thing is, when we open our hearts to seeing this side of the homeless, so often we receive so much more than what we could have imagined!

In helping others, we are helping ourselves out of our selfishness. Often, I feel that God calls me out of my comfort zone at times when I don't want to be called, and then blesses me more than I've ever been blessed in my life. This has been a constant experience in my life, especially in my work with the homeless. Being there for them is a continual invitation to let go of my own selfish and lazy habits, to expand my ability to love unconditionally, and to look beyond my initial impressions or prejudices.

It Starts with Yes

Just one example of this happened on a cold winter night in Denver. Only after I'd said, "Yes, I will go Lord," did what was to become fifteen inches of snow began to fall. It was still coming down hard when I got a text from one of my homeless friends, Clarissa — or "Glitterbear," as she was known on the street — asking if I knew where she and some of her other homeless friends could get some food, as they had not eaten all day. This particular day was our normal outreach day when we feed the homeless in downtown Denver, but because of the snow I didn't want people to chance driving, so I canceled it. I don't have a lot of people who donate food, so I had cooked up some brisket, potatoes, vegetables, and salad myself, before the snow came, and I was just starting to pack it up and put it in the fridge for another day when Glitterbear's text came in. The Knights of Columbus in Denver had given us a storage room, but before that, my dining room was the homeless storage unit.

I asked Glitterbear how many people were in each cubby under the bridge, and she said there were groups of three and four in each cubby, and there were four cubbies. I told Glitterbear to bring several people with her, to either catch the free mall ride or walk, and to meet me at the McDonald's on the 16th Street Mall in an hour. I filled two huge IKEA bags with Styrofoam to-go containers, silverware, and napkins, and then put on ski pants, boots, and a parka and started to make my way.

A gentleman coming out of the Capitol Building saw me hauling the bags and asked me where I was going and if I needed help. I told him I was fine, and that I was "balanced." He snapped a picture and sent it to my phone.

By the time I walked the six blocks to meet up with the group of under-the-bridge warriors, I was covered in snow, but when I saw their faces of relief, I thanked the Lord for getting me out of my comfort zone. The street kids later told me that they were able to eat for two days on the food that I brought them. Now if that doesn't warm my heart, I don't know what does. Saying yes not only can change your life but also the lives of those you serve. Glitterbear was the first person the Lord laid on my heart to take to Rome. Even then, he was already preparing the path, as that was several years before the Rome trip was ever a dream.

Finding the Right Person

When I first discovered how many young people were on the streets of Denver, I googled organizations that worked with homeless kids and young adults who were at risk. What I found was an organization called Stand Up for Kids, which only works with the homeless population that's twenty-five years old and under. I contacted them and told them I was interested in getting involved, so they signed me up and I went through several weeks of classroom training. I was then paired with an outreach director and continued my outreach training. Before long, I was leading my own outreach team every Tuesday and Wednesday evening. All the Stand Up directors and leaders would meet every Sunday night at a local church to serve dinner to the homeless youth and young adults. I stayed with this organization for six years before establishing the Denver Homeless Ministry.

While I appreciated the work Stand Up did, I saw that there was also such a need for those twenty-five and older, who to me seemed to be falling through the cracks, and I felt both the call and the need to minister to them too.

Sunday night dinners were more relaxed. A team of volunteers would cook and serve, and all the outreach counselors would grab a plate and sit with the homeless at different tables. This was a time to really connect and meet individual needs. When I started the DHM, I did not stop going to the Sunday night dinners, but I took it one step further by having Christmas banquets, prom nights, and masquerade balls for the homeless. On some of these occasions, especially in winter, the owners of the venues that hosted the event allowed the homeless to stay the night. We often used the Knights of Columbus Hall near Denver's cathedral downtown, and the only condition was that people had to check their weapons at the door — many carry knives, large pipes, or even guns for protection — and obey a mandatory curfew. The rule was that they had to be in by a certain time and could stay until a set hour the next morning. If they left in the middle of those hours, they would not be let back in. Once they were ready to go back out, their weapons and any other personal belongings they checked in would be given back and they were on their way.

The first of these events I helped to host was with Stand Up. I then organized two others on my own called 48 Hours, where fifty to seventy-five homeless young adults were able to get off the streets, and were provided sleeping bags, blankets, pillows, clothes, toiletries, showers, laundry services, and mega amounts of food with volunteers preparing and serving three full meals a day. Two years in a row a ministry called Christ in the City asked me to help train their volunteers. Together we had thirty to fifty volunteers spend forty-eight hours with those who came to the event. They planned movies, games, training lessons, and so much more. They even, on our last 48 Hours, coupled the last night with our Christmas program and honored me in a video presentation. Talk about tears! I was presented with a book put together by one of the volunteers, Christine, who is now a Carmelite nun in California, with stories of thanks from the street kids. This is something I will treasure for the rest of my life.

I first met Glitterbear, whose real name is Clarissa Lucas, on the 16th Street Mall. She was easy to talk to, she was warm and loving, and she was never rude or obnoxious to the outreach team, or for that matter to anyone else that I could see. At Christmas, Clarissa would bring her two children to receive the Christmas gifts that they had been wanting and asking for. To make sure we got all the gifts, I would organize a team that also partnered with other organizations working on the streets to compile a list of people who wanted to join the banquet, and gift ideas for each individual on the list. They needed to write down three things: a needed item, a wanted item, and a dream item. Once compiled, we would usually have fifty to seventy-five individuals on the list. I would then send out emails to all my contacts asking people to donate for one individual. All three gifts on the list were then bought, wrapped, and delivered for the Christmas banquet — three years in a row! One year Clarissa's daughter got the American Girl doll that she dreamed of, plus outfits. Although the joy on her daughter's face was enough of a thank you, the total joy and admiration on Clarissa's face meant the most. I believe she felt honored and respected because we loved and honored her daughter. We've remained friends all these years, through break-ups, moves, tears, and joys!

Clarissa's story is not unlike that of most people who live on the streets. While I don't know the details, I know from what she's told me along the way that she grew up with a mother she has described as "a verbal abusive drunk." She was sexually abused by someone close to her from the ages of two to four. Eventually, Clarissa was taken from her mother. After around three years, she returned and finished school, but right out of high school she got into a relationship with a man who led her down a path that ended with her living on the streets. She had her first child three years into that relationship, and she had a second child with the same guy a couple of years later. Clarissa was in this relationship for thirteen years, during which she's said that she was abused "physically, verbally, mentally, and emotionally." She finally mustered the courage to leave that guy, but by the time she did, her mother had been granted custody of her children and Clarissa stayed on the streets, visiting her kids as often as she could. By the time she came to Rome, Clarissa was in a new relationship and was starting to learn that love didn't come with cuts and bruises. She was starting to regain her self-confidence with the help of a local women's shelter and had started taking steps to get a job and secure an apartment for herself and her kids.

The Lord seemed to work in ways beyond our understanding. I truly believe he was planting seeds all along the way, even at those Christmas banquets, because Clarissa was exactly the right person to go on our first Rome experiment.

Starting from Scratch

In order to travel, Clarissa had to be released from probation, because she had a record. After speaking to her probation officer and seeing the efforts she had made in getting her life back on track, the officer said she thought the trip was the most fantastic idea she had ever heard of and believed Clarissa was the perfect candidate. The officer decided to end Clarissa's probation early so that there would be "no paper" on her way back through customs, and admired the fact that Clarissa was finally able to get housing about a month before the Rome trip took place.

When we took Clarissa, we had never done anything like this before, so we were starting from scratch. Needless to say, I had no idea what I was doing. When I first started organizing everything, the idea was to take a group of more than five homeless people, plus two chaperones and a chaplain. After a series of unfortunate and unexpected twists and turns, we ended up with just one homeless person (Clarissa), myself, and one chaperone. One guy couldn't get his passport because he was behind in child support, and one did not show up for any of our mandatory pre-Rome trip meetings, so finally I told him he couldn't go. The man's brother was very upset about it so he left a message on a friend's phone that "he could not wait" to get me alone in Rome. Yes, you guessed it, he didn't go either!

One other person in the group simply did not show up, so we lost the money for that airline ticket, which at that time was just over one thousand dollars. Four years after that trip, I met up with this guy and his counselor from another homeless outreach ministry called Dry Bones Denver, and I gave him his passport, which they told him would be kept for him in their safe. He apologized to me and told me he was in a very bad place at the time of the Rome trip, and just didn't know how to tell me. I believed him, as I had met and spoken to his mother prior, and how he survived his dysfunctional family life I cannot fully understand. Forgiveness is real!

As that first trip got closer, I had to make a decision about who would go as a chaperone, which was a hard decision to make. I couldn't justify more than two. After much prayer, I finally decided on taking Fr. Michael O'Loughlin — my spiritual father and a source of constant support — as our chaplain.

When we originally made our reservations at the hostel, we did so thinking that we were taking four guys, one girl, one chaplain, and three female chaperones. So, when it came down to just being the three of us, I had to readjust our hostel stay. They worked out our sleeping arrangements and the price that we paid, and we were able to get a room for Father Michael with five other guys, and a room for Clarissa and myself to share.

An Experience of Joy
When I said before that Clarissa was the exact right person to go to Rome, I meant it. With her, there was no drama — which as I discovered later wouldn't always be the case — and there were a lot of laughs, giggles, and fun times. She simply took joy in everything, and she was very laid back, which helped calm my own nerves as I tried to keep everything organized and on track.

Our first night was such an adventure, but it turned out to be a lot of fun. When we first got on the plane, Clarissa was nervous, knowing it was going to be a long flight, so we all sat close together. But once we were up in the air, she was fine, and she started to get excited to begin this adventure and to tell her family about every moment. The entire time we were there, Clarissa was upbeat, had a great attitude, and was excited to experience everything, even when she felt like her feet would not be able to take another step — which is something I appreciate even more in hindsight, as this upbeat attitude was not the norm during these trips! With Clarissa, we walked everywhere. Seldom did we take the train — only when we were out really late and the idea of walking back to our rooms was the last thing we wanted to entertain.

In the hostel, Clarissa and I initially had a room to ourselves with two sets of bunkbeds, a dressing area, and a private bath and shower. It was ideal, until our third night, when we came home late at night and saw we had two roommates who took the beds we had already claimed (this hostel had room service, sheets, and towels were changed daily). Clarissa woke them up and told them they needed to move to the top bunk because we had the lower ones already. All I could do was laugh because I didn't think I would have had the nerve to do that. That night Clarissa had a coughing fit that was so bad she had to get up and go into the bathroom for fear of waking everybody up. But it was too late; it woke us all up, as we weren't sure if she was dying or not. On the second night, we returned very late and found our roommates with headphones on, black gloves and masks, and their covers pulled up over their chins. We both started laughing so hard we had to shut ourselves in the bathroom until we could get ourselves under control. And then throughout the whole night if one started to giggle, we both started giggling. Even now I laugh when I think about it. Those girls did not return the next day.

We didn't see anything that first night since we got in so late, but Clarissa later shared that she still remembers the smell in the air when she first stepped off the plane. For her, even getting to our hostel and just walking on the streets was exciting, because she was taking in all the sights and sounds of being in a new place and in a country with such an ancient history. Like so many others who came to Rome, Clarissa didn't think she was worthy of it, and was shocked that she had been chosen. When we got there, she was pinching herself trying to convince herself that this was all real, and that she was, in fact, in a place she had always dreamed of coming.

For Clarissa, there weren't really any major "aha" moments or one defining memory of the trip. For her, the biggest impact came in experiencing the little things, and I think God spoke to her through the small details. Just being there, and soaking it all up, was lifechanging for her. As I look back, I think the most important experience was the absolute joy she felt — I'm not sure when the last time was that she had felt so happy, or had so much fun. I think Clarissa learned in Rome that life didn't have to be so hard, that it wasn't all sadness and pain; but that she could actually be happy, and that good things happened in life too. She took that discovery back home, and that new perspective has shaped the course of her life ever since.

I had been to Rome before as a regular pilgrim, but never leading a group. My first trip to Rome was after a car accident. I had received a payout and decided to take Resa, one of my friends from work. I fell so in love with the city that I knew I had to go back. I returned twice on my own — I love traveling on my own and experiencing the little shops, the pizza-by-the-slice restaurants, and the random churches in out-of-the-way places. I love sitting at a café having coffee, writing in a journal, and just talking to people. I made a fourth trip to Rome for Father Michael's birthday in 2013. He and I traveled together and stayed at an Irish pub, which helped us see that we could travel together for the good of others. Little did we know we'd be taking a homeless person with us the next time we went! After the first dream I had of taking homeless to Rome, Father Michael told me that if it's really from the Lord, I didn't have any choice if I wanted to walk in his path and say yes. So he agreed on the first two trips to go as the chaplain and chaperone. The biggest change of taking people to Rome was having to do all the planning: the passports, the flights, the rooms, the food, and snacks. All this was something I didn't think that I could do but did — by the grace of God, for real!

Like all of our subsequent trips, when we went with Clarissa, we spent a lot of time at the Trevi fountain, as this seemed to be everybody's favorite part. Attempting to throw a coin in the fountain with hundreds of people crowding around was both challenging and fun. Getting scammed at the Trevi is always an interesting experience for people who come for the first time. When a gentleman there offered Clarissa a rose, I tried to tell her not to take it, but she said the guy offered it for free, and then he literally chased her down the block to try to get money from her, so finally she threw the rose at him and yelled at him to get away from her. I thought we would die dying laughing about this later!

Clarissa's generosity moved me a lot on that trip. She never believed anything like this would ever happen to her, but from the beginning, she thought of others before herself. She had saved money to be able to buy gifts and mementos from Rome for her friends and family. Watching her buy a gift for every single person who meant something to her was so amazing. She bought gifts for her family, for her then-boyfriend, for Dry Bones, the ministry that helped her the most, and for a few other ministries working with the homeless in Denver. She spent very little on herself, which is something that has always endeared me to the homeless — they have such big hearts!

That year we decided to walk to every church on our itinerary, even to St. Elizabeth, which is located way up on a hill behind the Vatican. Clarissa was a trooper, because Father Michael walks very fast, and we both found ourselves doing a slight jog to keep up. She was in awe of the whole experience, like a little kid who unwraps a present and finds that it's the cool toy they've always wanted, or maybe one they never even asked for, and are now elated that it's theirs. In terms of the sites we saw, the main highlight for Clarissa was our visit to the Colosseum, which she had always dreamed of seeing but never thought she would. She spent a long time walking around, envisioning everything that happened there, and trying to soak in every detail. We also visited many other must-see places for first timers in Rome, such as the Vatican Museums and St. Peter's Basilica, the Pantheon, and Rome's famed Spanish Steps. Clarissa loved all of this, but she really got a kick out of seeing the small European smart cars buzzing around the city. Buildings and cars like this were things she said she had only seen in movies, so it was surreal to see them herself in real life. There was a deep sense of wonder on her face every day. She would light up as soon as we stepped outside, and her eyes were being opened to so many new things in Rome, but also in herself.

We also attended one of Pope Francis's general audiences. In future trips, we would get special front-row tickets where you could meet the pope, but that wasn't the case yet. Despite not being Catholic, Clarissa handled the audience very well — even though we got there early to get good seats and it was several hours before it was over, she never complained, and I could tell it meant a lot to her to be there. She later told me that it was amazing for her to be so close to a leader admired all over the world. As someone who never thought they would amount to anything or do anything of consequence at all, that experience of being so close to someone who was so respected made her feel important and special.

I had tried to organize some volunteer time with the Missionaries of Charity while we were in Rome. They have a house near the Vatican and I thought it would be nice for us, and for Clarissa in particular, to spend time serving homeless people there and getting to know the homeless situation in another country. At the time, I was told they were not in need of volunteers, but they said there was a service going on and that if we wanted, we could go inside their chapel and pray for them. I'm not sure what Clarissa thought about it all, but something totally amazing happened for me there, and I tell the story over and over again.

Adoration was going on — when the Eucharist is exposed on the altar for veneration — and we were sitting there when the priest came out and held up the host so we could all come up and venerate it one by one. At the time, I had a really bad knee and didn't think that I could kneel because if I got down on my knee I couldn't get back up, but I really wanted to. So I went up anyway and when I tried to get back up, a hand emerged from the priest's vestment, and he helped pull me up. I was told the priest never does that, and I had not said a word about needing help. I have grey hair now, but back then it was still brown, so it couldn't have been because I looked old either! At least, that's what I tell myself. Anyway, it was something beautiful that I will never forget. It was a God moment. To be honest, it was a little freaky at the time, but I knew the Lord did it and that moment remains special to me today.

When we were invited by the sisters to pray in their private chapel, neither Father Michael nor I knew how Clarissa would react, as asking our homeless guests to spend time praying was not part of our mission. But to our surprise, her response was, "Yeah, I want to stay and pray." That was surprising for us to hear, but amazing, as it showed just how open Clarissa was to new things. When a person is open-minded, the possibilities for what he or she can accomplish are pretty much endless, and Clarissa is no exception to that. She is still one of the most open people I've ever taken to Rome, and I think that openness is what allowed her to experience the level of joy and happiness that she did. She simply let herself be loved on for a week, and that love changed her life.

Another moment that made us laugh is when we bought these little squishy balloon balls sold all over the streets in Rome that are supposed to make a high-pitched squeaky sound when you throw them on the ground, then come back into the shape of a ball. Clarissa was very excited to be able to take them back to her kids, so she bought a few, but when she threw hers down, they didn't make the noise that they did when the guys she bought them from threw them. Fr. Michael explained that the guys were making noises with their mouths that we couldn't see, similar to ventriloquists. And yes, we got a big laugh out of that also, trying to re-create those noises!

Clarissa really appreciated being able to experience a lot of new foods and different kinds of pizzas and pasta dishes — and calamari. At one of our meals, I ordered a platter of calamari with marinara sauce. I was surprised, because the calamari rings were bigger than what we are served in the United States. Clarissa asked me what I was eating, and knowing she doesn't like fish, I just looked at her and flatly said, "Onion rings." She asked if she could try one and I said, "Sure." She took one bite and looked at me wide-eyed, and yelped out, "You lied!" She tells this story over and over again. Although she said it didn't taste as bad as she thought it would, it still wasn't an onion ring, and she didn't fall for that again!

Learning to See with Different Eyes

Once we got back from the trip, it didn't take long for things to start falling into place for Clarissa. Two days after we returned from the Rome trip, Clarissa moved into her apartment and took full custody of both of her children. Because she didn't want to remove them from the school they had been attending, she would ride the bus to and from school with them every day. Her son has now graduated from high school after playing on the football team and being Homecoming King. Not long after that, Clarissa's life took another new turn with a new relationship that has brought all her joy full circle.

I truly believe it was her experience in Rome that marked a turning point for Clarissa. She was already starting to get her life together, but having the opportunity to do something she never in a million years imagined she would do, and to travel to a place that seemed so far out of her reach, made her realize all the things that were within her reach at home. She started to see herself in a new way: not through the lens of her faults and failures, but through the lens of what she had accomplished and now realized she was capable of doing. I really believe she gained a confidence and motivation in Rome that changed the course of her life.

Several years after the trip, I asked Clarissa to write a blurb about her experience for the DHM website so we could advertise to potential donors. The one experience she recalled as having left a strong impression was meeting a homeless man in Rome who, she said, inspired her to want to help others who are in the same situation. Although the man did not speak English, he happily accepted the leftover food she gave him after one of our meals, and was humble in receiving it. In her reflection, this is what Clarissa wrote:

> Overall, my experience in Rome is indescribable. Having been homeless off and on in the past 14 years, meeting that sweet homeless man has helped me come to the conclusion that I want to help homeless, show them they can get off the streets, that they do have a chance and that there are awesome places to see. This world is full of negative, hateful, and judgmental human beings who look at homeless like trash and with disgust. I want to change that perception. Eventually I would like to make a difference with the homeless population. I want them to know there are people willing to help them see another part of the world, just the way my friend Tanya helped me see a different part of the world. When I came home, I wasn't the same selfish person I used to be.

God truly works wonders in those who are open to receiving his grace! Clarissa's view of the world, and others, changed because the way she saw herself had changed. It's funny how once we experience God's love and mercy, once we have an experience that brings light in the midst of our difficulty and darkness, we can't help but want to share that with others. To me, Clarissa is a shining example of that — of just how much a life can change thanks to having an open heart and a new perspective, how much love can motivate this change, and how generous a heart can become when it strives for something bigger than itself.

In Clarissa, I really understood how much a life can change when someone discovers who they really are and is seen as that person. I saw myself in Clarissa in so many ways: She was strong and yet weak, happy on the outside and sad on the inside, searching for love and thinking she had found it only to find it was counterfeit. She was always doing the pleasing and not being pleased, searching for something she didn't know how to obtain. That was totally me before I found Christ and gave my life to him and learned how to follow him. What I saw in Clarissa reminded me that I was not alone in my thoughts, feelings, and desires. They gave me an awareness of so many others out there in the same situation. Although I wanted to reach out to every single one, that would've been overwhelming, so the Lord placed certain individuals in my path, to be my friends and to possibly learn from each other. Having Clarissa go on the first Rome trip was the biggest blessing for me. We connected, we laughed, we supported each other. Her trip made me see the wisdom in God's choosing to do these Rome trips and picking her as the first one!

I also learned a lot about what it takes to lead these trips and to be in charge of someone else. I learned to stay organized, sometimes to the point of being anal with a time schedule, and I learned to be a bit more flexible with individual needs. While there, we found an internet cafe close to our hostel so Clarissa could call home at the end of each evening, and that kept her calm about leaving her family behind. I walked with her the first two nights and waited outside while she talked, then eventually I realized that she knew her way, she knew what she was doing, and I had to let go. I think that was good for both of us. Every trip after that, I built in free time for everyone.

At certain points Clarissa was getting very annoyed as we were walking around, and people were rude and bumping into her and knocking her around. She was trying to contain her cool but often found it difficult, so she asked if she could wear her headphones and listen to music as we walked. Perfect idea, as it worked throughout the entire trip. I learned from this experience that people from all walks of life have anxieties about "something." I didn't know how to deal with it, as I am not a psychologist/psychiatrist, and so I think I needed to learn to adjust to the needs of the people I was with by allowing them to use whatever means were necessary, except drugs or alcohol, to help them help themselves, whether it was headphones, smoking, or yelling at me to get it all out of the system!

On this trip we had a long layover in London. Father Michael took an earlier flight as he had to be back for church, and Clarissa and I took one of those double-decker buses into London and shopped and ate dinner, then rode the bus back and slept at Starbucks until it was time for the plane. That was an amazing adventure. I didn't think we could do it when the girl was explaining to us at the desk how many trains we would have to take and what the different train line colors were, but Clarissa said, "Hey, I'm used to taking the bus everywhere, I can do this." I totally had to trust that she could, because I am directionally challenged and will almost always turn right instead of left!

Clarissa wrote me a private message several months after coming back that showed me why these trips are worth it, despite all the hassle:

Made me cry cause I know God has used u to be in my life and I don't know if I ever told u, THANK YOU, thank u for being my ministry street mom, thank u for feeding us, thank u for a trip that I will never forget, thank u just for u being u but most of all I thank God for sending u … u will always be a big part in my life even though I am stable and hardly see u anymore, u are one of the very few people I will never forget and will remain in my heart forever. I love u Tanya Cangelosi.

You don't always receive these thanks yous for serving the Lord but when they come, so do the tears!

3

DERRICK

We Are Beautiful in Our Brokenness

In the Book of Isaiah in the Bible, Isaiah the prophet tells the people, "Fear not, for I am with you, / be not dismayed, for I am your God; / I will strengthen you, I will help you" (41:10). I can't tell you how many times I've experienced this in my own life — more than I can count! As I look back, it's obvious in hindsight that God was the reason I was able to get through some of my lowest points, even when I didn't really believe in him or care about the afterlife.

I've also seen this over and over again in my ministry. God works through people's lives even when they can't see it, or when they seem indifferent. In that sense, this passage could easily be applied to any one of my street friends, but it especially makes me think of my friend Tree. His real name was Derrick Yearout, but he was called "Tree" on the streets. A lot of people thought the nickname was because of his height, since he was tall and skinny, but the real reason was because he liked the outdoors so much. In fact, while we were in Rome — Tree was the second person we took — Father Michael, who also came along as a chaperone for that trip, bought him a plate with a painting of the Tree of Life. It was something Tree had really wanted, which to me said a lot about him.

Thinking about that plate now is kind of ironic, in a bitter-sweet way, because Tree died on December 26, 2020, after battling stomach cancer. To this day, Tree is the only person we've taken to Rome who has passed away, and when he lost his battle with cancer, he still had that plate from Father Michael. He was fifty when he died, so he was a little older than most of the other people who went, and even though he'd had some health problems for a few years, his death still came as a surprise. I had known that he was sick, but even though we were still in touch, I hadn't talked to him in a while, so I didn't know how serious it was. When I found out he died, it was a strong reminder for me that I need to be much better at staying in touch with the people I care about. To this day, I still regret that distance. I know from some of his last Facebook posts that he felt really alone when he was in the hospital, and I would have liked to be there for him more than I was.

Tree's life is one of those stories that once you hear it, you might be tempted to ask, why? What is the point of a life like that, spent on the streets and filled with abuse and hardship pretty much from beginning to end? Yet in every life there is beauty:

We just have to learn how to see it. I had to learn to see beauty in my own life, and it wasn't easy, but once I did, I started to see beauty everywhere, and I think Tree did too.

A Broken Past

I don't know too many details about Tree's past, but I do know that his parents met while they were both patients at the Pueblo Psychiatric Hospital in Colorado. Somehow, they were able to avoid security and had an affair that resulted in Tree coming into the world. At one point during her pregnancy Tree's mother tried to have an abortion, but she was prevented from doing it by the doctor at the psych hospital. So when Tree was born, he was given up to social services and put into foster care. Tree knew his father for a few years when he was really young but described their relationship as "a painful experience" in which he was constantly beaten and used. Tree's father first introduced him to meth. He was a painter and would sometimes make $1,200 a day for a job, but even though Tree helped him out, he never saw a dime — but he was paid with all the free meth he wanted. Later, Tree met a girl on the streets called Stump who helped him get clean and stay that way after she made him sit in a tent for four days smoking nothing but marijuana.

Even from a young age, Tree acted up a lot in foster care. When he was only five years old, he was admitted into the children's unit of the Fort Logan State Hospital, a mental health institute in Colorado. He stayed there for two years, but said it was like "hell," so he ran away when he was seven. He got picked up right away and was readmitted until he was ten. That's when he was moved into Colorado Christian Home (CCH), which is a place that helps children and families in difficulty. Tree stayed there until he was fourteen, when he discovered the street crowd in downtown Denver. For the next four years, Tree was in and out of CCH but spent most of his time on the streets, because he said he felt safer with the street kids than he did at the home. According to Tree, his street friends "taught me how to live and they were more like the family I never had."

Tree moved out of CCH when he was eighteen and started living on the streets full-time, panhandling to get by. Sometimes he would stay at a local group home called Urban Peak, but the rooms were small, so he spent most of his days with the Gutterpunks. He rose through their ranks fast and would often steal food from local grocery stores to feed himself and his street family. Tree never really went to school or had any sort of structure in his life, but he was a quick learner on the streets, and he soon became a protector and provider; the younger kids looked up to and depended on him.

I met Tree on the streets about six years before we took him to Rome, and I was amazed by how the street kids trusted him. They usually shy away from older street people, but Tree was different. Youth who hung out on the 16th Street Mall downtown relied on him to help them find much-needed items for street survival. At the time, there wasn't a kid on the streets that didn't depend on him, and that left an impression on me.

Like most everyone else we took to Rome, I didn't really know Tree that well, even though I'd seen him around a lot. But I knew he was the one who was supposed to go because I got that gut feeling I always get from the Lord telling me, "This is the person I've chosen!" I don't know how to describe that feeling; it's a deep intuition that I get, and I just know in my heart that this is the person God wants to go. When it was time to choose the person for the 2015 Rome trip, I had been thinking for weeks about who to take, and then one day while we were doing outreach on the streets someone came up behind me and gave me a hug. I didn't know who it was, but at that moment I knew beyond a shadow of a doubt that that person was to go to Rome. When I turned around, it was Tree.

Tree was very excited when I asked him if he wanted to go, but he wanted me to pick somebody else. In his mind, he wasn't worthy, and there were a lot of young people out there that needed this more than he did. I asked him if going would raise his opinion of himself, and he said, "Just being asked raised my opinion of myself." And then I told him, as I tell everyone, "I did not pick you, the Lord picked you — I'm just the messenger!"

That year I had actually wanted to go to Ireland for the trip, since we had gone to Rome the year before, but I believe, deep down, the Lord wanted Rome to be the point of destination. After much prayer and reading my Scripture, I could not get Rome out of my heart. I ran the idea of going to Ireland by my board of directors, and they said no, and that they believed it needed to be Rome and people who donated for the trip also believed in Rome, so that was that! Rome is such a magical city of faith. Mine grows every time I go, and I've seen a twinkle in the people who have gone, too. During Tree's trip, he questioned Father Michael over, and over, and over again about becoming Catholic. Prior to this trip, all he talked about, to us, was the Catholic conspiracy theory. So, all in all, the Lord knows what he's doing!

It's Never Too Late for Change

Prior to going to Rome, Tree started working at a local restaurant to earn some spending money for the trip. I found out later he could only volunteer there as he was on Supplemental Security Income (SSI) and was not allowed to actually work, so the gentleman who ran the place paid him some cash under the table, but it wasn't very much apparently. Tree continued to do this until his health failed him.

The woman who runs the luggage shop at Denver International Airport donated a huge piece of hard-sided spinner luggage for the trip. That was a random and unexpected offer, but she had heard about what I do and wanted to help. So, when

I offered it to Tree, he asked me what my luggage looked like, and I said it was just a green and brown tapestry, soft-sided sale luggage that I picked up in Rome on my first trip when I over-bought. The luggage that the woman at the airport gave us was purple, so Tree asked if he could switch with me, which I did, and later donated mine to a young runaway who we were able to help return home to another state.

A friend from church, Chris, gave me enough money to buy Tree some clothes, which were not easy to find as he was six-foot-four, and extremely skinny. I found three pairs of pants and several shirts, and that's all he wore the whole trip. Chris also gave me one hundred dollars to exchange into euros to give to Tree for personal spending money. So Tree did have his own spending money, and was able to buy his own cigarettes and his own souvenirs. On our last day he asked me for an extra ten euros, which I gave him from my own pocket, so we didn't draw on DHM funds.

Before Rome, we tried to get Tree some dentures, because he had no teeth. I had worked with a nonprofit dental clinic to get Tree a full set of dentures, but he missed his appointment. He rescheduled, but then never showed up for his fitting. He told me it was because they weren't ready, but I had my doubts — so I called him out for lying about it and told him I was fearful about taking him on the trip, because if he was going to lie to me about something like dentures, I didn't know if I could trust him on the trip. He apologized and called the dentist, and later went in and got the teeth, but he never wore them. He said that for more than forty years he learned how to eat without teeth, and that he was afraid he wouldn't be able to experience the different foods he wanted to try if he wasn't able to chew with the new teeth. That sounded fair enough to me!

Tree also struggled with anxiety, so he promised to make an appointment with a doctor to get meds to take when he was flying. He met with the psychiatrist a week and a half before the trip and was given Valium for the flight. He said his medical doctor would meet with him after he returned for an evaluation.

In the months before we left, Father Michael and I met with Tree several times to go over the list of things we would be doing while in Rome and asked for his input on what else he'd like to see or experience, after giving him a book of Rome that had details on some of the main sights. He was still a little confused about what we would actually do in Rome, but he had some ideas about what he wanted to see, some of which I allowed and some I vetoed.

About three months before we went to Rome, Tree got off the streets, which was a huge step for him. Colorado Coalition for the Homeless was able to get him an apartment, and with his SSI check he was able to pay rent. The apartment was considered a permanent placement for him as long as he continued to pay his rent on time. From this point until the very end, Tree continued to help those living on the streets, offering them his couch when they were in a bind, but especially by his example of improving his life.

Overcoming Anxiety

Once we set off, Tree was very excited, but also very nervous. He experienced high anxiety on the flight over, and he was also struggling with very high nicotine withdrawal. There were a lot of times during our trip that he needed to stop for a cigarette. On our flight from London to Rome, things seemed to go much smoother because he had leg room in an exit isle. He seemed to have a higher level of anxiety and nicotine craving on our return flight, but having a three-hour layover in Philadelphia helped.

While in Rome, the place we stayed at was a bit farther outside of the city than the year before, so we had to use public transport to get around most of the time. That ended up being a good thing because I hadn't realized before the trip how physically handicapped Tree was from his anxiety, and sitting on a bus gave him time to calm down. When we got to the hotel on the first night, we laughed because there was a small room with two single beds and a tiny bathroom that Tree and Father Michael had to share, while I got the master suite! I didn't plan it this way, it's just how things worked out, but we all found it hilarious. Every time I would plug in the blow dryer and my curling iron, I blew a fuse. After a few days everyone figured out that it was me blowing fuses, and we would laugh every morning when you could hear my name being shouted down the hall. (Well, maybe I'm the only one who found that funny.)

Despite never having a formal education, Tree was actually a very smart guy, and the ancient traditions were the things that touched him most in Rome. He looked up everything on our itinerary before we came, so everywhere we went, he knew something about it. That amazed me. To this day, I think he's the only person we've taken who's done that. So, Tree was able to spout off little trinkets of information throughout every place we visited, and that made him feel good.

One thing that did become an issue on this trip was the fact that Tree did not take a shower for the entire week that we were there. It was gross, and no matter how many times I told him that he stunk, he would not shower. So, the next year I added a clause into the contract for the person going that they are required to take a shower every day, and the girls who come have to wear shirts that cover their leggings, if they choose to bring them, and they are not allowed to show bra straps or cleavage. Some of that might seem like a no-brainer, but when you think about it, that is how a lot of young adults dress, not just homeless, so I ended up having chaperones sign the same agreement.

It also really annoyed me that Tree would flirt with the gypsy girls who beg for money in the streets. Officially they are called the Roma or Romani people. They are an Indo-Aryan nomadic itinerant people who live mostly in Europe, often on the outskirts of big cities, and do not assimilate into the culture in which they live. Over the years, they've gained a reputation for engaging in illegal and shady activities. While not all of them live this lifestyle, in Rome they are considered thieves. You'll often see old ladies hunched over, using a cane with one hand and holding a worn-out cup with the other asking people for money, and then a minute later the same hunched-over old lady will stand up straight and run across the street to get to a new location. A lot of the younger women also sit with kids, but not all of them are theirs. It's rumored that the women will trade kids in the mornings based on who's going where. They are also known for committing petty crimes like pickpocketing on subways and in crowded places. Because of this, they often face a lot of prejudice and are treated rudely, especially by the locals.

There was one episode with Tree and a gypsy girl that was, while frustrating, also sort of endearing. Father Michael was a better witness to this moment than I was. According to his version of what happened, the woman came up and asked for money, and no matter how many times they said no, she wouldn't give up. Father Michael said he kept eye contact with her the whole time, and the two of them were both being "very stubborn," and that drawn-out stubbornness eventually became humorous. At a certain point, the woman couldn't stop smiling as they all dueled it out to see who would cave first. Father Michael believes it was that smile that won Tree's heart, and from that moment, he was a goner. He continued to flirt with all the other gypsy girls who came up to beg throughout the rest of the trip.

Tree said he was hoping to offer them a better life, either by giving money or trying to create an interest so he could get together with someone later. He and I ended up having an argument about that. I told him the gypsies were not homeless, that they had a place to stay, and you can't just take people in no matter who they are or what country they're from. He of course disagreed and said that if you give a homeless person a chance, and if you give them a home, let them stay with you for a while, that could make a difference in their lives and lead to real change. I said I agreed with that, but that's not usually how it happens. I think Tree found this out later after he got back home, because he would allow lots of people to stay with him, and all but a few robbed him blind. Then he told me that he understood what I was trying to say. Tree had a big heart, he liked to help other people, but he also liked to argue, and I would get impatient. Father Michael always appreciated his perspective, though, and described him as "a thinker and an analyzer." No matter the topic, Father Michael genuinely enjoyed hearing his thoughts on things.

Discovering Beauty

Tree's relationship with Father Michael was very special for me to watch during that trip. The two of them really bonded, and that relationship continued even when we returned home. Tree would contact Father Michael periodically with questions, or for big things like when his mother died, and other important details in his life. This is one of the reasons I trust in the power of a chaperone. I don't connect with every person who goes. As much as I'd like to and as hard as I try, it's not always the case because of our personality and life experiences. But generally a chaperone will connect in areas that I don't, and that's why I find them so valuable. Father Michael was very special in that regard. Throughout the trip, no matter what anxieties or questions Tree had, Father Michael was able to calmly answer them and bring him back into the reality zone when he got off-centered. I actually believe that was the greatest asset of this trip, and in the long run, I think that is what made most of the difference in Tree's life.

I'm sure we will never know all of the fruits and the benefits of this trip for Tree, but he constantly questioned Father Michael about becoming Catholic — he wanted to know how soon he could do it! One clear benefit from this trip was that Tree discovered the beauty of real friendship and meaningful relationships.

In the middle of the week, we attended one of Pope Francis's Wednesday general audiences. We were up at the front, close to where the pope sits, but not in the handshaking area. So Tree walked around until he found a spot up front that was really close to where the pope was shaking hands and blessing handicapped people. Since Tree was almost seven feet tall, he saved a spot in front of him so I could come and be that close too. That was pretty endearing, and it showed me how much Tree really thought about others.

Tree was impressed that during the audience, the pope did not turn anyone away, but was trying to connect with as many people as he could. Tree later said that "it was like a warm feeling inside when I was near him." I think seeing someone as important as the pope show special attention to the poor, the sick, and the disabled really struck a chord for Tree. To see people like him who are usually ignored and invisible to most of society get so much love, it was like the pope saw how beautiful they were in their brokenness. Seeing that helped Tree to understand that he was special too, and that regardless of his past and the things he had done, his life meant something — *he* meant something. I think he finally started to see the beauty in life, and in himself.

Later that day we decided to go inside of St. Peter's Basilica, but Tree said he didn't want to go in and that he was going to go stand off to the side by where the guards were and smoke. At that point, Father Michael said I needed to pull rank, so I went over and told him that he needed to go inside, and that he could stand at the back of the church the whole time if he wanted to, but that he had to stay for at least fifteen minutes, and I would be watching him. How's that for control? Well, fifteen minutes went by, and I couldn't find him, so I assumed he had just gone outside to smoke, and I went back to looking around. When I was done, about forty minutes later, I went outside to look for him, but I couldn't find him anywhere. At that point I panicked and thought maybe I had been too hard on him, and he had wandered away. I sat there for a bit wondering what to do, and then to my surprise Tree came out of the basilica. He had been in there the whole time, and said it was the most phenomenal place he'd ever been in his life. He took dozens of pictures, touched everything he could possibly touch, and was glad I made him go through it.

Tree told me that he had a young son, but never had the opportunity to bond with him. After the Rome trip, Tree's son was brought over for a visit and Tree got to show him all the pictures he had taken. He said that was the first time they really bonded, because his son loved the pictures from Rome. I don't know how close they were before Tree died, but if the only thing that came out of the trip was bringing those two closer together, that would have been enough in my eyes!

The day we volunteered with the Missionaries of Charity left a big impression on Tree. They have a little soup kitchen and shelter right next to the Vatican, and they allowed us to come work with them for a day. We spent the day doing laundry and washing dishes. The sisters serve thirty women at their shelter and give a nightly dinner to the men living on the streets. There is another shelter for men just around the block, right across from Holy Spirit Church (Santo Spirito in Sassia), which is about two steps from the Vatican and does Masses in English every week for pilgrims and other visitors.

At one point during our time there, a nun named Sister Anne Marie took Father Michael and me down to the basement to rinse, wring out, and hang sheets to dry while praying the Rosary, and Tree was put to work in the kitchen. Tree was so engrossed in his dishes that he didn't know that Father Michael and I were taken downstairs. When he looked up and saw that we had gone he didn't know what to do, and started to get nervous. The poor sisters who were with him thought he was going to have a panic attack, so they let him sit down and have a cigarette in the women's smoking area. But he was totally fine when he saw us come back upstairs, and got back to work. I make a lot of mistakes on each of these trips and there are a lot of lessons I learn. This time, I learned that I had to communicate better, especially when I'm dealing with people who have high anxiety!

Working with the Missionaries of Charity was a highlight for all of us, but especially for Tree. He felt like he was making a difference, especially because he got to interact with homeless people. He helped in serving the meal to the men and was in a totally different section than where Father Michael and I were doing laundry for the women. I think it made him feel like he was contributing, and the nuns also really liked him and gave him a lot of attention. They knew that he had been homeless, and I think they took that into consideration in their treatment of him. I remember afterward Tree told us that although he didn't speak the language, he understood from the men he served that they were thankful. This trip made absolutely clear what a big heart Tree had, and how much he really wanted to help other people. He was always so aware of what they needed, and I think being able to serve the homeless made him feel like he was giving back. The trip was for him, yet somehow, he kept finding ways to make it about other people.

Coming Back Different

Right before the Rome trip, Tree said that he'd been living the same way for so long, he didn't think he'd ever be able to change, and would still spend his time looking out for his street family when he got back as he had always done. And that's exactly what he did, though he did make some huge changes in his life. He got his own apartment, and his attitude changed. He was more positive, and he really made an effort for the people who were important to him. He always let friends crash at his place either until they moved on or ripped him off, and that's when he would kick them out and refuse to let them back in. He was always looking for a way to give back, and he even volunteered at some places. Despite all our debates and all the ways that he annoyed me sometimes, he was a really good guy, and he was there for his street family until the end.

Looking back on his trip later, this is what Tree had to say:

> I like the Rome trips. I believe that they are inspirational and a way for the homeless to get a once-in-a-lifetime opportunity to not only have time away from their life of misery and drug addiction, but it's a way for the Catholic Church to help do good in spreading the word of the Catholic Church. I had a wonderful time with you guys in the room, and it has changed my life forever so yes, I think you should keep the trips going and changing people one day at a time.

Reading notes like this never gets old. The best thing I can ever hear after a trip is when the person who went says their life has changed, and you can tell from looking at them and what they're doing that it's true. That's God's wisdom at work!

Despite all the interest he showed during the Rome trip, Tree never did become Catholic in any official way. He did tell me sometime later that he had been going to church on and off since we returned from Rome, and that he had stayed in touch with Father Michael. The relationship between those guys was one of the best things to come out of that trip, and even if that were the only positive thing to come out of it (which I know it's not by a long shot!), then it was worth every toil and trouble along the way!

When Tree died, he only had a handful of family left. His mother had died a few years before, and I know he had his son and a brother. Beyond that, I'm not sure, but it seems like his family wasn't able to afford a funeral. Tree died on December 26, and a couple of weeks into the new year I was in touch with his brother, who said they still hadn't made funeral arrangements. That got me curious, so I asked around with some friends who work for a few of the other outreach programs in Denver, and one of them told me that Denver has a fund to pay for cremations for indigent folks. In Tree's case, I'm still not sure exactly how everything played out, but I do hope he was eventually laid to rest with the dignity he deserved.

When I think about Tree and his story, I'm reminded of something that was said about St. Benedict Joseph Labre: "He became a pilgrim, traveling from one great shrine to another, living off alms. He wore the rags of a beggar and shared his food with the poor."*

Despite all the difficulties in Tree's life, he was blessed, and I think he died a happy man. As anyone who has lived through any ordeal, we, looking in from the outside, might say, "I could never live through that." But when you're the person going through a situation, you simply go through it not realizing that you can't go through it, if that makes sense. I also had my own battle with cancer when I was younger, and when I got my diagnosis, everyone around me was devastated — but for me it was just something I had to endure for a time. It wasn't easy, but I made the best of it without thinking about how others who were looking in from the outside felt. I think the reason family and others had

---

*"Saint Benedict Joseph Labre," Franciscan Media, April 17, 2021, https://www.franciscanmedia.org /saint-of-the-day/saint-benedict-joseph-labre.

such a harder time with my cancer was the same for Tree: They didn't know how to fix the problem. But I don't think Tree saw his challenges as problems. I never knew him well enough to say whether he looked back on everything that happened to him with gratitude for making him the person he was, but I think he looked back with acceptance. Especially after Rome, I think his attitude changed; he no longer resented what his life had been or who he was, and he had begun to see the beauty in all that brokenness. There wasn't any big "aha" moment, but there was change, and it was real.

Tree had a way of staying positive even when he was hurting. Yes, he had a few down moments, but for the most part he tried to stay upbeat. Only the Lord can put that kind of positivity in someone's life. The beauty is that I believe he believed and trusted God to the very end. I suppose if there's one lesson Tree's life offers, it's not to judge a person by their looks or what you perceive might be happening in their lives. Get to know that person, pray for them every single day, and when you get a chance to help them move to the next level, you'll be ready!

4
SHYLA

We Can Receive God's Forgiveness — and Learn to Forgive Ourselves

In the Gospels, when Peter asks Jesus how many times he should forgive someone who sins against him, Jesus responds, "I do not say to you seven times, but seventy times seven" (Mt 18:22). Of course, I've heard this passage a lot at church, but I don't think I really knew what it meant until I met Shyla Montoya.

Shyla was the third person I took to Rome, and hers was by far the most difficult of all the trips I've led. More than anything else, it made me question what I was doing and why I was doing it, and I probably came closer to pulling the plug on the whole thing than I ever have. It was awkward, it was humiliating, it was tense, and it was painful. I didn't quite realize it at the time, but Shyla was in a bad spot. She was angry, and all that anger seemed to come out at once while we were in Rome. Yet what has happened in her life since, and to see the young woman she's become, to this day brings me to tears. I can only describe it as a miracle, the work of a God who knows more and sees farther than I ever will.

Holding on to Anger

Each of the Rome trips is different. We tend to follow a similar trajectory in terms of the touristy places we visit — the Colosseum, the Pantheon, the Vatican Museums and St. Peter's Basilica, and any number of other sites that draw millions of visitors to the Eternal City every year. But each trip is set apart by the person we take, and the experience he or she has.

Most of it is fun, but not all of it is easy. Typically, during each trip the person I bring at some point has a meltdown. With all the anxiety over new people and experiences, the travel and being around the same people all day every day — all of which would be enough to put anyone on edge, let alone someone who's been homeless, who struggles with anxiety, and is used to doing things on their own time — it can all be a bit much. Emotions run high and can tend to blow up like a volcano. In my experience, the eruption is inevitable and usually involves some screaming and a fair amount of tears. On every trip I know it's going to come, I know it's going to be awful, but I also know that we're going to get through it, and that once the tension is released, the rest of the trip will go better.

With Shyla, the entire trip seemed to be a meltdown from start to finish, and there was no sense at all that it would let up or that we would get through it. From the moment we stepped onto the plane, it was DEFCON 1; Shyla was on edge, and I became the target of what felt like razors of pure hatred perpetually pointed in my direction. It was as if all the anger she had ever felt in her life up to that point all came out in one agonizing week, and I bore the brunt of it. Yet through Shyla, I learned humility and I also eventually learned what Jesus meant when he told Peter to forgive. In some ways, I think we both did. But we had a long road to get to that place.

Shyla was twenty-two when I took her to Rome in 2016. When I first met her on the streets, she was around fifteen or sixteen, and was very shy. She wasn't actually living on the streets because the Urban Peak outreach program had given her a small apartment with a bed and a refrigerator, but it was in an unsecure and dangerous building where people would often get shot or raped. Shyla hung out with the street kids a lot, so I met her when we would go out to bring food and toiletries. I could never be sure if she liked me or was laughing at me as she plotted my demise. I tried hard to connect, to help meet the needs she was reluctant to share. We served dinner every Sunday night and Shyla would show up, get a plate of food, and sit with her friends. She totally ignored staff, or maybe it was just me. Those are really the only interactions we had. I hardly knew her before asking her to go to Rome, and even when she came out, she rarely talked to me. She's definitely one the Lord chose — I wouldn't have.

I was so excited when I first felt the Lord lay her on my heart for the trip in 2016. I felt a deep connection to her since we had both experienced traumatic events during our childhoods, and I thought I could relate to her, but I was wrong. I was so wrong. I couldn't relate to somebody with a bad attitude, because the Lord by then had changed my attitude about my own past. My past has made me who I am because the Lord allowed me to see that my past does not define me, but Shyla wasn't at that point yet.

Shyla was raised by her great-grandparents. She never knew her father, and she spent her early childhood going back and forth between her mother and her great-grandparents until she was six. That's when her mother died, and she went to live with her great-grandparents full-time. She stayed with them until she was fourteen, when her great-grandfather died. His death broke her, and she decided to run away from home. She ended up living in a group house for a while before eventually deciding to go back, but when she tried, social services told her she couldn't return because of her great-grandmother's age and because of the trouble she tended to get into. So, she was put into foster care, but she ran away again and got by couch-hopping with friends before eventually returning to the group house. Shyla eventually got back in touch with her great-grandmother, who she always called "Mama," and decided to go back to school. But when she was eighteen, her great-grandmother died, and Shyla started to drink and steal to get by. Eventually, she pulled herself together and landed a job working at Auntie Anne's pretzel shop and was able to get an apartment of her own.

I always say that it's not me who chooses the people who are supposed to go on the Rome trips, but it's God who shows me who he has chosen. When he put Shyla on my heart, I thought it would be the best experience ever in her life. In retrospect, I think maybe I was thinking what an awesome person I was to listen to what the Lord had to say by laying somebody on my heart, and I was going to change that person's life. But that's not how the Lord works. He asked me to do something, I said yes, and then it was his turn, but I wasn't really giving it to him because after all, this was all about me! Taking Shyla to Rome taught me to "let go and let God" — you know that old cliché. I did let go and it turned out to be the worst trip I've ever had in Rome. Seven trips and I seem to keep making the same mistakes, yet the Lord still used me. What a great God we have!

Learning to Trust in His Plans

In the lead-up to the trip, Shyla received her passport with no hassle at all. I didn't have to talk to a judge or parole officer before applying for her passport, as I had to do with a couple others that went on a Rome pilgrimage. Yet as we were going about our preparations, I knew something was different. Her attitude toward me changed as we were shopping for Vatican-appropriate clothing, luggage, and much-needed phone adapters, and I couldn't figure out what was up. I would try to help her by finding cute outfits that were donated and that would be appropriate for the places we'd visit, but she would reject anything I held up and would find things on her own. And when we finally did leave, she had not packed any of the church-appropriate clothing she had shown me prior.

At the time, Shyla told me she was just going through a rough time. I really did not know or believe that rough time could last through the entire trip to Rome and for a month or so after when I stopped all communication. This was a very rough point in my life. I'd come to believe that maybe I really didn't listen to the Lord. So much self-doubt made me want to rethink any future trips, but still I told everyone that it was the Lord who chose Shyla, and the Lord would work everything out. And every night I said: "Lord why did you do that to me? You left me hanging. You made me look like a fool and feel like gum on the bottom of somebody's shoe!" I felt in my heart that the Lord told me: "Be patient, follow my lead, and I will never leave you. I love you." He never did leave me, and I know in my heart beyond a shadow of a doubt that he loves me very much. And the weirdest thing is that the Lord gave me a love for Shyla that I didn't know was in me. He has a way of doing that; somebody you think you could never love becomes the one person that is so important to you that you pray for them every night, which I did from the very first night I met this girl.

In Shyla's own words, before the trip she was "struggling for food and clothes, and drinking a lot, I was lost. But something hit me. The Holy Spirit, I think." Can your prayers for someone you barely know make a difference? It always amazes me, the life-changing events the Lord has set in motion for each individual whom he has chosen for these Rome trips, but Shyla's will always be a special story simply because of the drastic changes she made after coming back.

For Shyla's trip, we had a travel agency out of California called the Catholic Travel Centre that loved what the Denver Homeless Ministry was doing and wanted to help. They paid for our hotel and a rooftop dinner on our first night in Rome, they provided tours and our final dinner at a restaurant with live singers who walked around the tables, singing special songs for each person. I felt like I was in heaven for all that was provided!

We were supposed to have another chaperone come with us, but this person canceled at the last minute due to personal issues, so it was just Shyla and me. Our first night at the hotel Shyla did not want to eat, despite having reservations provided by the Catholic Travel Centre, so she went to her room to be on her phone. We shared a room to keep the cost down, but when Shyla got there, she thought our beds were too close together, so she kicked them apart and broke my converter. I honestly didn't know what to make of all of this, especially since it was only night one! She seemed to hate me from the moment we got on the plane through the entire trip. She had wanted a window seat, so I got her a seat a couple rows up from me because I wanted an aisle seat. At one point I walked up the row and asked her how she was doing, and she half-yelled back, "I'M FINE!" A lady who was sitting a seat away from her asked me if she was OK. I told her it was her first time flying, so maybe she was nervous. Well, that went over like a lead balloon with Shyla, she told me to never speak for her again. Lesson learned!

On our first tour of the Vatican, she avoided me as if I was evil. She wouldn't sit with me on the tour bus, and she wouldn't walk with me on the ground tours. People asked me if we were together, but I never knew what to say because it was so awkward. During one of the ground tours, a gypsy woman kept walking up to Shyla and jiggling her cup to ask for money. Shyla eventually had it, and at one point full-on yelled, "GET AWAY FROM ME!" The rest of the people who were on the tour with us moved back away from her. A little old man that was on the tour with us came up to me and said maybe she needed some cold water. I looked at him, and I said to pour it over her? He laughed and gave me a couple of euros to go in and buy her a bottle of water, which I did, but in truth, I just wanted to go hide somewhere. I could not see how the Lord was involved in this at all. I'm shortsighted! Yet looking back, I see the Lord had a plan. He wanted to show me how to love no matter what, and to allow Shyla to grow up.

Despite everything, we still had a fantastic tour at the Colosseum. We loved our guide, and Shyla seemed to relate to him very well. But whenever we went back to the hotel, she wanted to talk to her friends. She was on her phone 24/7, video conferencing and chatting with her friends, as her aunt had paid for her extra phone usage while she was in Rome. After that trip, I imposed limits to phone usage for the others. I made it a rule, because I wanted people to experience the trip on their own, not spending time talking or on social media.

During one of our dinners, we had a reservation at a place where an opera singer walks around the tables singing to individuals. Whenever the singer came to us, Shyla would turn her back until the woman went away. This was also the dinner where Shyla took a picture of me drinking a glass of wine and sent it to her aunt telling her that I was an alcoholic. I got several emails, as did the travel company, about this from her aunt. When I asked Shyla if she'd like a glass, she said, "I don't drink in other countries!" When we got back from Rome, Shyla sent another email to me, the owner of the travel company, and his sister, who works there, complaining about how horrible the trip was and how awful I had been. As a result of that, they opted out of helping with any further trips, although they did pay for the hotel and one dinner during the trip that we took the year after.

Shyla also wore no bra for most of the trip, and she carried a bill for five euros with her that she told her friends she would give to an Italian guy to take his shirt off. Hearing her tell her friends this over and over again on the phone and posting it on Facebook, I finally got upset and told her if that if she got arrested for soliciting, I would let her butt rot in jail and I would go home. Of course, she got mad at me.

You may be tempted to ask me, "Why did you deal with it?" I dealt with it because I knew deep down in my heart it's what the Lord wanted. When Shyla would go back to the hotel room, I walked some of the back streets by Termini Station, the main train station in Rome, to find small open churches where I could just go in, kneel, cry, and pray.

I do want to make it clear that I take full responsibility for this trip. I believe it was my fault things turned out the way they did because I didn't take a chaperone. When the second chaperone canceled because of personal issues, I thought it would be fine because I knew Shyla and so everything would be OK, but as a result of our experience, I never went on another trip without a second chaperone, (except for the trip we took in 2020, which happened as a result of a fluke mistake, and is something I would regret.)

Seeds of Change

The turning point for Shyla, not in terms of the trip, but in terms of her own path, came on the day she met Pope Francis. He holds a weekly general audience on Wednesdays, and that year we had special *baciamano* tickets that got us to the front row on top of the platform where he was speaking. The word *baciamano* literally means "kiss the hand," so the tickets are called that because the people holding them get to meet the pope. In the past, it was traditional to kiss the pope's hand when you met him, but of course Francis doesn't like that, so I usually just do a handshake or something and give him pictures of the street kids my ministry helps.

Getting Shyla ready for the audience was another task in itself. When we had gone shopping prior to the trip, she said she didn't need anything, that she had clothes. I asked her to take pictures and message me so I could see if we needed to add anything. She did and there was only one little dress that was strapless, so I said she probably wouldn't be allowed in most places wearing that without a little jacket, which I did buy her, and one of my friends donated a sweater hoodie with fur around the hood for her to take along. As it turns out, the only dress she brought from all the pictures she sent me was the strapless one. The rest were very clingy, and there were some long, skimpy knit dresses. They took up one little corner of her suitcase and there wasn't much more in there. She only brought a pair of slip-on shoes, not the walking shoes she was asked to bring.

The day we were supposed to meet the pope, Shyla chose to wear the strapless dress. I told her she needed to bring a jacket. She argued with me, and I just walked out the door. When we got to St. Peter's Square, I showed the guard our tickets, and he said to me, "Tell her to cover up." I looked at him and said, "You tell her," so he said, "Cover up!" She put on the sweater hoodie with the fur around it and had to wear it in eighty-some-degree heat while sitting in the sun the entire time. And she continued to look at me as if I had grown horns. I felt so evil yet vindicated.

While we were waiting for the pope to come by for our turn to shake his hand and receive a blessing, several Hispanic people on pilgrimage standing behind us asked Shyla if she could get the pope to bless all their rosaries. She took them and lined them up on her arm, about twenty-five rosaries, and once the pope blessed them, she handed them back to the pilgrims. I believe that meeting with the pope was a pivotal point in Shyla's life. It seems to me that something special had happened to her; there was a different radiance. It didn't affect how she treated me nor how I felt about her by that time, but I could tell something was different after that.

When we went to pick up our pictures from the Vatican photo office after meeting the pope, it surprised me to see how big her smile had been. Prior to this, the only time I'd really seen her smile was when we were crossing the street in the rain and my shoe slid and I went right down on my butt, which sent Shyla into a fit of laughter. But in this photo I saw something in Shyla that told me, in my heart, that the Lord was beginning a mighty work in her which has continued to this day.

Unexpected Transformation

Things were still tense after we came back, and Shyla's attitude was still so bad that I eventually had to cut off all communication. Not only did she write the travel agency to complain about me, but everything she told them, she told to all our mutual friends. Only one of them chose to no longer be my friend because of this trip. When I got home people said, "See now, do you still believe the Lord told you to take her?" And I could only answer, "Yes, I do believe the Lord told me to take her." And I had peace because I knew in my heart the Lord was going to change Shyla's life and was changing it in ways that I couldn't yet see.

And in changing her life, my life was changed as I learned to trust him even more.

Before all communication was cut, Shyla told me she was leaving Denver to move to New York, where she got a job working in a hotel. I didn't know this at the time, but she was lying, and was still in the Denver area. We had had no communication at all for two years, when I heard from her again in a message she wrote to me on Facebook. In her letter, Shyla said that she had joined an evangelical church and was baptized. My jaw nearly dropped through the floor, and I was bawling so hard I could barely see straight. I want to share that letter with you, because I believe it speaks to the miracles that God was working in Shyla, even in the midst of our most difficult moments. The Lord knew I needed encouragement, and I believe this letter came from him:

> Hey Tanya, I'm probably like the last person you want to hear from, but I do want to apologize from the bottom of my heart when we went to Rome. I was still angry with life and none of that was your fault and you didn't deserve my attitude. I turned my life around, dropped all the negative people that were in my life. As soon as we came back my life started to turn around slowly into a beautiful [one]. It took me so long to apologize because I had to forgive myself first. You don't have to respond if you don't want to, I just want you to know that I do apologize. You're an amazing person and I just want to thank you for letting me see a different part of the world and to experience something different. Have a blessed week.

Not only did she send the letter to me, but she also wrote an apology to the travel agency and posted it on Facebook:

Hello, I don't know if you remember me, my name is Shyla, and I had the opportunity to go to Roma in 2016. I want to apologize from the bottom of my heart for all the drama, manipulation, and the lies, I was in [a] bad place at that time in my life, but I do want you to know that I really did appreciate that I had the opportunity to go to Rome. I do appreciate you so much for helping me with that. Rome has changed my life, I'm a different person, I have faith in Christ. My life is different, I'm different. Miss Tanya can testify to that because we are on good terms. Just a thought, this program is something that can turn somebody [from] who they think they want to be into someone different, it's really a life changer.

Now if that's not a changed life, I don't know what is! Shyla and I have stayed in touch ever since she reached out, and now we talk on a weekly basis, if not more. She'll write to me with prayer requests for a specific situation, or just to say hi. She has found a family at the community church she attends who has basically adopted her. She's lived with them for the past couple of years while looking for jobs and dealing with health issues.

A few years ago, Shyla started having some health trouble. She was having seizures, which I believe she'd always had, but they started to get worse. She was diagnosed with epilepsy and the doctors also found tumors in her brain. It was a scary moment when I found out all this was going on, and I prayed for her every day. The people she has been staying with, who she calls her "spiritual parents," have been amazing. They have been at her side the whole time; they haven't missed a beat. Thankfully, Shyla is doing well and continues to recover from a brain surgery she had for a brain bleed related to the tumors. Shortly after the Rome trip, she began taking medication for her epilepsy, which

I think has helped and will continue to help her turn her life around even more.

For me, I believe the miracle of this trip is not only how Shyla's life has changed, but the lessons we both learned. I had to forgive her for being a pain in the butt and by doing so, we both learned to forgive ourselves. That can only be accomplished by the Holy Spirit, and it certainly was!

Even though I swore Shyla's would be my last trip, and even though the Lord and I argued about this, and he had to convince me that I was to go on and do more trips, he did, and I love him even more for it. He changed my heart, and he gave me a future vision that I didn't know I had. I can tell people with more certainty than ever that this was the Lord's doing not mine; that if he wants it, he'll put it together and he will figure it out.

5
MELANIE

We Find Our Dignity in the Heart of the Father

While Shyla's story is impressive and inspiring, not every trip results in drastic, 180-degree changes. But every person who has gone to Rome has been changed in some way; each one of them came back different, and I truly believe the trip helped set a new course for their lives. Some of that has been very visible, as it was in Shyla's story; for others, such as Melanie Medina, the changes were more subtle, but just as deep.

Melanie was the fourth person we took to Rome, and her

trip was so different from Shyla's. Melanie was thirty-eight when she went in 2017, so she was a little older than most of the others we took, which makes a big difference. In some ways, it makes the trip easier, at least in terms of the emotional roller coaster that each one tends to be. Call it maturity, call it wisdom, personality, whatever you want, but older people who come experience the trip differently. They might have some things that they are dealing with, but there's less drama, at least in my experience. That was certainly the case with Melanie; she was sweet, calm, and very easy going, and she had a very deep appreciation for being there, and for seeing everything that we did. And this was exactly what was needed after Shyla's trip! I didn't know then how things were going to turn out with Shyla, so I took this trip as a leap of faith that it was something the Lord really wanted, but I was still a little shell-shocked, and Melanie's joy throughout the whole trip put me at ease. We had a lot of fun together, and that was something we both needed.

Changing Habits

I first met Melanie when I was handing out snack packs on Capitol Hill, near the cathedral downtown. She was a regular at our feeds, and over years I came to know her and love her and respect her. Even when she was at her worst, I still saw a deep beauty in her. I believe I saw her dignity because of the Father's heart in me — because he had allowed me to see the beauty in myself when I was at my worst, and in many ways, Melanie reminded me of a younger version of myself.

When I think of her, I'm reminded of chapter 10, verse 13 of Saint Paul's First Letter to the Corinthians, when he says that "No temptation has overtaken you that is not common to man. God is faithful, and he will not let you be tempted beyond your strength, but with the temptation will also provide the way of escape, that you may be able to endure it." For so many people on the streets, the pain they experienced leads them to self-medicate through sex, drugs, alcohol, and so on. Melanie was no different.

Before going to Rome, Melanie had been living on the streets and was struggling with alcoholism. She grew up in an alcoholic family, and from a young age she was often the one responsible for taking care of her parents and cleaning them up at night. There were times when her father got so drunk, she had to guide him to the bedroom and tuck him in at night. When she was fifteen, Melanie left home and went to stay with her older sister, who was also an alcoholic. She started hanging out with gangs and eventually got involved in an abusive relationship. Melanie had two kids with the man by the time she was nineteen, but eventually had enough of the abuse and left him. Not long after that she started a long-term relationship with another man and had her third child with him, but after the baby was born, she began to drink heavily. Eventually she broke up with that man too and put herself through rehab. When Melanie got out, her second ex-boyfriend, the father of her third child, offered to get her an apartment and pay rent so that she and the kids could stay together while she got on her feet. Well, it wasn't long before he went back on his promise, leaving Melanie on the streets while her kids went to stay with her mother. At first Melanie tried to stay sober, but she started drinking again when the camp she set up with a friend was raided and all of their stuff was taken. They moved camps and would store their food and belongings in trees so mice and rats couldn't get to them. Like many women who end up on the streets, Melanie suffered untold abuses. She was beaten too, once until she was almost unrecognizable. The year before we went to Rome, she started having severe problems with her feet and could barely walk. Just wearing shoes was painful. She never got a diagnosis for what was wrong, so she just bandaged her feet and gave up shoes altogether and walked around in socks when she could manage to stand up. After a while, her feet started to heal, and it was around that time that Melanie and her boyfriend at the time, Christopher, decided together to make a change and get off the streets.

When it was time to start thinking about who to take to Rome for the 2017 trip, I did what I always do, and started praying about it and asking the Lord to show me who he wanted to send. I told him that I knew he had someone in mind, all he had to do was let me know who it was! I knew it was Melanie when I saw her on Easter Sunday. I was heading down to Stoner Hill to help Stand Up for Kids serve dinner, and on my way I stopped by the Knights of Columbus Hall, where we had a storage room, to pick up some supplies. When I pulled into the driveway a couple walked up to me. At first, I didn't know who it was, but as they got closer, I saw that it was Melanie and Christopher, and I was shocked. I didn't even recognize Melanie because she hadn't been drinking for over a week and her whole appearance had changed — she had a different look on her face and there was a shine in her hair. Everything about her was different, and before I even knew what was happening, I found myself blurting out, "Do you want to go to Rome?" Prior to that moment, I had told the Lord that if I didn't find somebody that day, I would have to scratch that year because of how long it takes to get passports and plane tickets. I really had no idea that Melanie would be the next one to go, and the fact that this happened on Easter made it even clearer and more special. The Lord always knows what he's doing!

She was able to get her birth certificate rather quickly, and we applied for a passport that week. As we were applying for the passport, she got a call from the St. Francis Center in Denver saying they were able to get her housing, but she had to go that day, and we were blessed enough to get in and out and in a very timely manner, even though there was a line of people waiting at the post office. It all sort of came together, which is a miracle in itself!

Next, I sent out an email asking if anybody was willing to help buy Vatican-approved clothing, meaning things that were appropriate to travel in, enter churches in, and to go inside the Vatican itself. Fr. Dave Dwyer, who by then was director of a Catholic multimedia site called Busted Halo, answered the call and we went shopping! It was so much fun allowing Melanie to pick out clothes, and not worry about the cost. I don't think she had ever been able to do that. She was always thinking of other people and making do with what she had, but this was about her, and I don't think she'd ever felt that special before.

When we finally got our plane tickets, Melanie, our chaperone Christine, and I headed to the airport, but there was a moment of panic. As we were waiting for our American Airlines flight, it was announced that that flight would be canceled. We were told we could go home and come back the next day, as they were going to rebook us on another flight. After all the excitement building up to this trip, that was heartbreaking, so Christine went up and told them this was unacceptable, and they had to do something better than that. So, they put us on a flight that night to Dallas and put us up in a hotel. When we arrived at the hotel, the agent wanted to know if we could all stay together, and we said no as our luggage had already gone on and we had no clothes. So, we each got our own room, a voucher for dinner and breakfast, and another voucher for snacks at the airport. It ended up being a really fun night. American Airlines totally came through!

Discovering Dignity

Normally we've arrived in Rome late at night, but for this trip we got there around eight in the morning, which was perfect for us. The Catholic Travel Centre had again provided the hotel for us in Rome, and when we got there, we were told our room was ready. Then Melanie, in classic fashion, said with no filter whatsoever, "No shit, it should have been ready last night!" I was taken aback at first, but all of us laughed, even the woman working reception who agreed, "That is very true!"

When we got to our room, we had three very plush single beds, a huge window overlooking the streets, and an extremely large bathroom and dressing area. As we were unpacking some of our luggage and looking out the window, Melanie laid on her bed and said, "Can we take a nap?" We immediately said yes, and we all ended up sleeping for about three hours. It was great. Then we got up and went to explore some of the city as we were looking for a place to eat and buy ponchos. It was one of the most relaxed first days I'd ever had on one of these trips, and I think the others appreciated the fact that we eased into it.

I am extremely directionally challenged, which immediately became an issue. A few days after arriving, Melanie made the comment as we walked out of the hotel, "Tanya why do you always turn left when we always go right?" I have no idea why, but I did it every single day and all we could do was laugh. I've never laughed so much in Rome as I did on that trip. Melanie was such a joy to travel with. One time we got lost for quite some time, even though Christine was using her GPS. I had no idea where we were or if we'd gone around the same block more than once — I am that challenged. At one point, Christine got teary-eyed and I was afraid that I would be mad at her because she got us lost. It could have been a tense moment, but that's when Melanie chimed in and said, "Tanya doesn't know right from left, why would she be upset with you because we were lost for a moment?" That totally changed the atmosphere and made us all laugh again. I was impressed at how Melanie read and diffused the situation so fast.

One of our favorite days was in Assisi. We had so much fun that day. Our first stop was the Basilica of St. Mary of the Angels, which has a tiny little chapel inside called the Porziuncola. I've completely fallen in love with it, as has almost everybody I've taken. I read something years ago saying that there are more angels in that tiny chapel than there are in the entire world. I don't know where I read that, but wherever it was, I tell everybody that and I think they try to spend some time in the chapel to see if they can feel the presence of angels. I don't know if the angels are really there, but it's nice to think about as you're sitting and praying.

The basilica was built up around the Porziuncola, or "Little Portion," which was renovated by a young St. Francis of Assisi and is where he first felt and understood his vocation and decided to renounce the world in order to live in poverty among the poor, thus beginning the Franciscan order. Not long after, St. Claire of Assisi, a friend of St. Francis who belonged to a noble family, joined him, as she felt called to live the same penitential life, and eventually started her own order called the Poor Clares, who live the same meager lifestyle as the Franciscans, but who are cloistered. This little chapel holds so much faith and history, and Melanie seemed to embrace my love of the chapel more than any of the others.

To get into the town of Assisi itself, you have to go up a large hill. When we got to the town, Melanie, Christine, and I saw this tiny little path that went up the backside of the houses to the very top of the hill. It wasn't easy to climb, which was Melanie's idea, but it was a great experience. When we got to the top, the views were absolutely breathtaking. I had not gone to the top with any of the others we've taken — we just did it that one time — but it was absolutely worth it. We spent a lot of time walking around taking pictures and talking before actually touring Assisi. That was a highlight for Melanie and a beautiful experience for all of us.

Melanie truly enjoyed everything we did on that trip. There was not a museum, monument, fountain, or even crowd of people, that Melanie did not become overjoyed at. Although there were highlights — she loved the art museums we saw and the Colosseum — most of her delight was just being there. Seeing Rome through her eyes was a great experience, a joyful experience. I'd been to Rome several times by then, and as much as I appreciate it every time I go, everything was new for Melanie. She was seeing all of this history and beauty for the first time, and she was soaking it all in. She never thought she would ever have an experience like this, so she was in constant wonder at every new thing we saw or place we visited, but she had a great sense of humor too. Even when we went to see the pope, we weren't that close, but we were on the platform up by where he speaks, and at one point Melanie got right up by the front and stood on a chair and yelled at the guards to get out of the way so she could take a picture of the pope. Who couldn't laugh at that? We all did, even the guards, and we got some great photos.

The day we went to see the pope was Melanie's birthday. She turned thirty-eight that day, and even though she wasn't very religious, I could tell she really enjoyed being there. We had hoped to get the same *baciamano* tickets that we'd had the year prior with Shyla, but unfortunately that wasn't possible this time, though Melanie still really enjoyed it anyway. Being that close to someone important and respected was cool, and I think it helped open her mind a bit. I remember that she thought he was very friendly, and she was impressed by how he interacted with some of the kids. There was one boy the pope was greeting near where we were sitting, and when the pope came by, he ruffled the boy's hair, and took some pictures with the family. Melanie was moved with how the pope treated them. I remember her saying that he acted as if he were one of them, and that was important for her to see. Pope Francis had just returned from a six-day visit to Colombia the day before, so he had to have been exhausted. Melanie was impressed that he would still make time to be with all the people who came to see him that day.

Later that night we celebrated Melanie's birthday with a special dinner provided by the Catholic Travel Centre. Elise also joined us for that, which was fun. She has a history with my ministry and knows a lot of the street people we take, so it was fun for her to see Melanie again, but in Rome instead of Denver. All food, snacks, and dessert were provided as part of the dinner, so we had a great time! For the entire trip that was the only time that Melanie drank. And possibly a little too much, but she was fine when we went back to the hotel to sleep. I never monitor what the people we take eat and drink. Obviously, no drugs are allowed, but if they want to have wine with a meal, I leave that up to them. I make it clear at the beginning of every trip that I'm no one's mother, and I trust them to make their own decisions. For the most part the people we've taken have respected that.

When the waiter at the restaurant found out it was Melanie's birthday, he gave her a full bag of biscotti to take home. But instead of keeping the whole thing for herself, Melanie decided that for her birthday she wanted to hand them out to the homeless sleeping outside at the Termini train station, near our hotel. Elise came with us and acted as our interpreter as we talked to people and gave them Melanie's birthday biscotti. That was a highlight for everyone on the trip — the homeless were grateful for the biscotti, and even more grateful that someone bothered to stop and talk to them! I think it was important for Melanie too as a way of giving back — she had been in their position, and she had received so much with this trip, and the apartment she got right before leaving, I think she wanted to share that with other people somehow and handing out those biscotti to people who were still on the streets was her way of giving them a piece of the joy she was experiencing, it was her way of telling them that they, too, were worthy of good things.

I remember Melanie being struck by the difference between

homelessness in Rome and homelessness in Denver, mostly in the fact that in Rome the homeless were actually allowed to sleep more or less wherever they wanted, even train stations, which is something homeless people can't do in Denver. If they lay down at a train station in Denver, they are woken up and in not-so-polite words, asked to get up and move along. We were only in Rome for a week, but Melanie's impression was that homeless people were treated better in Rome, and that they were calmer. In her mind, this is because they had "the right to rest" without getting bothered or shooed someplace else.

Melanie did not bring any spending money for the trip, which not only meant that she had no money for souvenirs — she is also a smoker, and for the entire trip could not buy one package of cigarettes. I'm fine with lending money for a keepsake or two, but cigarettes are one thing I refuse to provide. They must bring their own money for that. But that did not deter Melanie whatsoever. She did what a lot of homeless people do, which is *skype*. I don't mean call someone on the internet; *skyping* in street jargon means scrounging around on the streets for discarded cigarettes that haven't been fully used. She looked for them everywhere, and whenever I would see an almost unused one, I would grab it for her. Even to this day I have to stop myself from picking them up!

I honestly had so much fun on this trip, it was the first one I hated to see end. But end it did and her boyfriend was very glad to see her come home. Melanie was excited to go home and sad to leave Rome all at the same time. She could hardly wait to get back to share her experiences with Christopher. We had planned to take Christopher the following year, but that fell through, and they ended up breaking up later anyway. But I think Rome had a lasting impact on Melanie — it showed her what she could accomplish, being alcohol free, if she really wanted to. That in itself is enough to change a life!

Breaking a Pattern

One of the biggest impacts the trip made on Melanie's life was in her relationship with her children. She talked about them constantly while we were in Rome, and I could tell she felt like a failure, and that she hadn't been there for them in the way she wanted to be. Melanie later had another boyfriend, with whom she had a new baby boy a couple of years ago whose name is Christopher Bear. Being a mother is important to her, and in a sense, she got a second chance at motherhood when Christopher Bear came along. No one is perfect, and Melanie still has a lot to work through, but she is a different person with a different opinion of herself now. I think she loves herself in a way that she didn't before, because she saw what she can do, what she is capable of if she puts her mind to it. I think she sees her own dignity now and can hold her head up high if she wants, and I don't think she ever felt like she could do that before.

In a little blurb we asked Melanie to write to DHM sponsors who pay for the Rome trips, she said something to the same effect:

> Do I think Rome trips should continue? Yes, definitely! It gives young people who fell in bad times hope, something to look forward to. When I was asked, I saw not everyone gave up on me and that God wanted me to see the light and remember that no one is perfect, and he don't [sic] give up on his children. This is an experience of a lifetime. It gives us hope and makes us remember we are worth it, we are loved and we can get back up even from the point when we believe we can't. Yes, I would love to see the trips to Rome continue. Thank you for the experience of a lifetime and knowing that we are worth it, thank you Tanya and the people that donated money to help us go, thank you for believing in US that we could change.

Melanie reminds me of Ven. Matt Talbot, who lived from 1856 to 1925, and is considered a patron for alcoholics, even though he is not a saint yet. He was born in Dublin and his father had a hard time providing for the family, so at the age of twelve Matt started working as a messenger in a wine bottling company. It wasn't long before he began abusing alcohol, which he did for almost fifteen years before he finally made a pact to never drink again, when he was twenty-eight. He went to confession and started attending daily Mass. The first few years of being sober were hard, and it was difficult for him to avoid the places he used to drink at, but he did it. He also made an effort to pay back people he had either borrowed or stolen from while he was drunk. Eventually, Matt developed a deep prayer life and joined the Secular Franciscan Order. He worked as a builder for the rest of his life and gave up meat for nine months out of the year. He also regularly prayed the Rosary, read Scripture, and donated to foreign missions, despite the fact that he only had a modest-paying job. He died while on his way to church on Trinity Sunday, after forty-one years of abstinence from alcohol.

To this day, many addiction clinics and youth hostels are named after Matt Talbot. Even though the piety he had later on in his life is admirable, only fellow alcoholics who have stopped drinking are able to fully appreciate just how hard those first few years of sobriety are, and the kind of willpower and discipline it takes to stay clean. Matt had to take it one day at a time, as does everyone making this journey, and I believe Melanie is on her own version of this path right now.

After returning home and having her baby, Melanie realized her relationship with the child's father was not good, and neither was moving forward with their lives by being in that relationship, so she had to move on with her life. That wasn't easy for her, but I believe she was able to do that with dignity, maybe for the first time in her life, which is something I hope helped her to break the pattern of unhealthy relationships in her life.

Melanie has been through a lot, and there were many points along the way where she wanted to give up on herself, but she kept going and is in a much better place today. She's turned her whole life around, and I think Rome helped her to do that. Rome showed her that no matter what your past looks like, no matter what regrets you have, what you've endured, or the many ways in which you failed, you still have value, and you are still worthy of being loved. Rome showed her that as bad as life gets sometimes, good things can still happen, and it's possible not just to survive, but to thrive.

As I've said before, one of the things that really helped me in my own personal journey was when I found St. John Paul II's theology of the body series, which he wrote in large part to defend human dignity — the value that each person has just because they are them, and not because of their race, religion, wealth, power, or social status. Even though she still has a lot to sort out, I believe Melanie gained a real understanding of the "dignity of the Father" simply by being asked to go to Rome and being given all the chances to make her own decisions. She was lost for a while, but now I truly believe she has found what she needs to take the steps that she has to, and that is something I can only thank God for!

6

M&M

We Can Break the Cycles of the Past

In Saint Paul's First Letter to the Corinthians, he gives a clear warning to the people of Corinth: "Do not be deceived: 'Bad company ruins good morals'" (15:33). I see this so often in street life: People who left to their own devices are kindhearted and caring, but are in a bad place and often get stuck in unhealthy cycles because of the people they hang out with. For those who are homeless, their street family is their lifeline; the streets are a dangerous place, and without friends and a community to watch your back, they can be deadly. Anyone who ends up on the streets or spends a lot of time with that community has something going on — there's a reason they ended up there. I've always seen my ministry as a tool to help reach these people, especially youngsters, before they get so caught up in that lifestyle that extracting them from it becomes difficult, if not impossible. At least, that's always been my hope. I'd like to spare as many of these kids as I can from only more pain that they will inevitably experience the farther they go down this road. Whether any of that works or not, of course, doesn't depend on me. As the old cliché goes, I do my best and let God do the rest!

That has certainly been my approach to my street friend "M&M," who asked that I keep her identity anonymous for the sake of her daughter. She was the fifth person we took to Rome, and she was only twenty-three when we went in 2018. Of all the people we've taken, I know probably the least about her past. I know she was born in an apartment in Dallas and raised by her grandmother, who had Alzheimer's, and that she started couch surfing as a teenager and experimenting with drugs. She spent much of her adolescence in and out of jail, and eventually ended up on the streets in Denver. M&M described her situation on the streets as being oppressed by men. For women on the streets, young women in particular, it's common for them to attach themselves to an older man who provides protection, but there are certain expectations that come with that. Whatever M&M's exact situation was, I'm not sure of, but I do know she would describe her experience of street life as one of freedom; freedom from materialism, and a place where she learned how valuable friendship and love are. She always said she found "supportive and encouraging" communities who embraced her love of art and skateboarding, and who cared more about who she was than what social class she belonged to.

She found all of that liberating, which is not uncommon for

people on the streets, but it's a deceptive sort of freedom, because all the while you are enslaved to other things, whether it's drugs, sex, alcohol, or something else. I believed for so long that I was happy and "free" before I attempted to take my life, and that was a wake-up call to me that it was all a charade. I don't think M&M ever experienced anything like that, but I do know that when we took her to Rome, she wanted to get a job and get off the streets. She was excited to see the world and had dreams of going to art school and starting a family, and Rome was a unique opportunity for her. I didn't know then that it would actually take a miracle to get there!

Change of Plans

When I first asked M&M if she wanted to go to Rome, it was during an outreach night with Stand Up for Kids, and she said no. I was surprised, because most people I ask are excited about it, and M&M seemed indifferent, but I figured it was her choice, so I let it go.

That year was the first time we ever went as part of a group, and it was also the last. A few months after getting back from Melanie's trip, I bumped into a man named Paul Spotts, who runs Catholic Young Adult Sports (CYAS) and who I'd met through some of their events. He told me he wanted to take a group to Rome, and that he wanted to invite a homeless person to travel with them. I was immediately nervous, because of all the complications involved in taking a homeless person, from getting travel documents to new clothes, dealing with their records so they can pass customs, and not to mention all the anxiety! But in the end, I said yes, because I remember how Shyla at one point said she wished she was in a group. For some reason Shyla was under the assumption that she was going with a group, and I have no idea where she got that from. She apparently had a lot of assumptions on that trip! In any case, I decided to give it a try.

I still didn't have anyone to go, but I saw M&M again one night when I was out by Stoner Hill, so I told her I would ask her one more time and that if she said no, that was it, I would never bother her again. She said she would think about it. Well, a few days later she contacted me and said she wanted to go. I told her to meet me at the Starbucks on 16th Street Mall so we could go over the details. Well, the day came, and I sat there for quite a while waiting for her, but she didn't show up. I finally texted her and told her that I assumed she did not want to go and was leaving. She texted me back and said she was sitting right behind me! I had no idea how long she had been there. I thought to myself, is she not a brat or what? Since she came, we went over everything and I made her sign the contracts that I make everybody sign before we go regarding actions, weapons, hygiene, permission on getting background checks done; basically, getting all of her information. There is also a waiver of liability to sign for the DHM and for me. After completing that we set a time to meet for passport pictures. For that, I usually set a time for people to meet me at Walgreens first, so I know they're really going to show up, and then we head to the post office to get the passport information done. So far so good.

As part of the preparations for the trip, Paul's group held several fundraising events that M&M was also asked to participate in. She agreed to meet with his group for an initial meet and greet, and she helped serve a Friday fish dinner which was used to raise money for the trip. I think that was a wake-up call to some of the other people in the group, because I remember how during one of those dinners, M&M was helping serve drinks and offering people seconds. After the last round, when she was clearing plates off the table and scraping them into the garbage, I noticed she was eating fish off some of the dirty plates. At that point I told Paul's group it was time to sit down and eat. They didn't get it at first, but they understood once I told them what I saw. We hadn't realized that M&M had not eaten in quite some time, so I think that was an eye-opening experience for the group, most of whom had never worked with homeless before.

Things went pretty smoothly up until the time we flew out. M&M did all that was required of her. I took her shopping to get shoes and clothes that she needed and wanted, and we also got a large piece of American Tourister luggage that was donated for her trip. But in the middle of all that, we also had to deal with M&M's record, because if we didn't get that cleared up, it was possible M&M wouldn't be able to go at all.

A Clean Slate

I did not know when we started this process that M&M had a rap sheet a mile long. She had numerous offenses that she had constantly dodged court dates for, but in order for her to get her passport and be allowed back into the country, we had to get all that dealt with. And that led to what I can only describe as a miracle.

As we were going through the process and dealing with the courts, M&M was given a hearing for potential jail time. Originally the court said she would have to serve ninety days, but the assistant district attorney said he thought he could get that down to nine days in jail with time served and probation. Well, the day came, and M&M stood before the judge, listening to all the charges listed against her. The judge asked her about her life and the whys that allowed her, a twenty-three-year-old, to be living on the streets. He questioned her about past and present addictions. M&M said she was clean and off drugs, but occasionally slipped up with alcohol. Then the judge asked me to speak on M&M's behalf, so I got up there and told him that by that point, I'd known her for about four years and that in the time since she was asked to go to Rome, she had gotten housing vouchers for a local motel until better housing came along and that she had started working at the Purple Door Coffee shop. I told him the change I saw in her in those months was not my doing, but that of the Lord, and that this same thing had happened to each person we took to Rome with the DHM.

The judge then told M&M that if she had an adult willing to come to court and stand by her, she had better not disappoint me, but do everything in her power to change her life. He then told us how his grandmother had also raised him, and when she was on her deathbed at eighty-two, he made it back in time to hold her hand and ask her, "Grandma, did I make you proud?" and she said, "Yes you did, very proud," and then she died. We were all crying at that point. Then, the judge did the most amazing thing I've ever seen a judge do: He dismissed M&M's whole case! All of it. Gone. He asked the police, who were standing behind us with handcuffs, to leave, and he pointed to me and told M&M, "Make her proud!" By that point I was sobbing, I was a complete mess. As we were walking out the door, the judge asked us to send him a postcard from Rome. No jail time, no probation, nothing — case closed! I had never before seen anything like it. For anyone who's ever been in the system for anything, things like that just don't happen.

No Change Is Overnight

We were all on a high from that experience for a while, and I was convinced that God was already beginning something good in M&M's life, but there was a lot still to come, and I didn't know then just how challenging this trip would be.

The day we were leaving for the airport, I met Paul at the hotel where M&M was staying with her voucher. From there, M&M and a few others would be riding to the airport with me. Well, when we got there, we found out M&M had been kicked out of her hotel room for some reason and a woman in the complex had let M&M stay with her. That meant M&M didn't have a place to stay when we got back, as far as we knew. I was disappointed, but it served as a reminder that there is real grace present in every one of these trips, but change doesn't happen overnight. It takes time to break those cycles and past habits and start creating new patterns in our lives, especially when addiction is a factor. And M&M was no exception to this rule.

Once we started making our way to the airport, things went well. Paul took us to dinner before we boarded the plane. There were twelve of us altogether, and everyone was Catholic, except M&M. That was hard for her, as everyone wanted to love her to pieces and show her the love of Christ. I think it was a little overpowering at times. Not that anyone wanted to continually witness to her about the Church or anything, but M&M just wasn't used to being loved on that much. On the plane she was nervous, but one of the group members, Mary Lakey, and some of the others reached out to her and helped make it a comfortable trip for her.

A Stop in Paris

That year we stopped in Paris for two days before going onto Rome. We stayed in an Airbnb, which was a little crowded. M&M shared her room with a couple of the girls, and when she opened her luggage, the girls in the room almost fell over; it smelled so bad it was unreal. She had brought all of her clothes with her, and she had nowhere to leave them: dirty, clean, new, old, all of them. The girls didn't know what to do about it, so they tried to be good sports and just did nothing.

Many of the places we went in Paris were places that Catholics would be totally interested in, and we had Mass every day, as we had a priest with us every place we went. Now that I look back, if I were a non-Christian, or even a non-Catholic, I would've felt like I was with a cult. And that's exactly what M&M said. She was an atheist, so she wasn't interested in all of this church stuff. I think it's my fault as I didn't think all this through before we went. I actually feel sorry for her now, even though it was an experience that she'll never ever have again, being able to go to both Paris and Rome, and Assisi. But it was hard for M&M emotionally, which made it very hard for the rest of us emotionally. When they had daily Mass, I told M&M she did not have to attend after the first one, and she did not. Then we had Mass at about every church we stopped at. I can't even imagine what it would been like for me before I was still a non-Christian. I don't know if I would've gone in the first place, so the fact that M&M stuck it out says something.

We also did a boat trip in Paris at night, which was amazing. I enjoyed that it was cold out, and it was fun to watch people in Paris come out for picnics all along the Seine River. There were hundreds of them, in groups dancing and singing. It made you want to be a part of that.

When Twelve Is a Crowd

When we got to Rome, our apartment was behind the Vatican, and it was much bigger and better laid out with more bedrooms and fewer people per room. M&M again shared with a couple girls in the group, Raquel Mora and Mary Lakey, and by then her luggage was so bad that I almost threw up when I walked in. The girls told me they had to keep the door open, so I sprayed her luggage down. Afterward M&M came to me and asked if I could do something with her luggage because it really smells. That was so sad because I think she was embarrassed about it, and I felt for her. We did have a washer and dryer, and I don't know why the laundry just wasn't done then. I think it was because we got very busy after that, so it was dealt with later.

At the end of every night, we would have testimony time and talk about our highs and lows for the day, and one night M&M chose to open up. I wasn't there because at the time I was at the store buying stuff for breakfast, but I was surprised when I heard it, because it was a really big step for M&M to take, and I was impressed. Well, I learned another lesson here, and this is one of the reasons I will never travel in a group again, because M&M's story was repeated by one of the group members to a friend of a friend who then posted it on Facebook. When M&M read it, she went ballistic, because she had not given any rights to that story. She had every right to be upset, and I believe the person who posted her story later took it down. No one meant any harm, but needless to say, I made it clear that nothing like that could happen again!

I said earlier that the people who come to Rome usually have at least one major meltdown, but M&M had many, and I think it was because being around the group so much was overwhelming. It wasn't anything specific — it was just a lot for her. I honestly think she was doing her best, but it was just too much. She was fine when she and I hung out for a couple of days alone, but when we had to hang out with the group, she rebelled. I told her we came with a group, so we need to hang with them at least part of the time, and she didn't like that one bit. One significant meltdown happened the day we went to Assisi. She and I were going to take the train while the rest of the group rented cars. Being a part of DHM, my board and I didn't feel driving was the best option; we felt it was safer to take the train, so that's what M&M and I did.

M&M was very excited about doing that. The morning we left, I was waiting at the door for her to come down, as the rest had already left because their drive was going to be almost an hour longer than our train ride. When M&M got ready, she was wearing a darling little dress and had boots on and was ready to go, but I made the mistake of telling her that after this trip, we were going to have to spend time with the group. I was waiting for her at the door and couldn't figure out what happened to her, so I went in the room, and she was back in bed and was wearing her night shirt and sweatpants. I asked her what was going on and she said, "I don't want to be with the 'group' anymore!" I told her she didn't really have a choice and to get out of bed and get dressed, otherwise we'd miss our train. Again, she said no, so I raised my voice and said we had to get going and to get up. She told me to quit yelling at her, so I lost my temper a bit and actually started to yell, telling her that this is what yelling sounded like. It wasn't my proudest moment of the trip, but it worked, because M&M got up, but she refused to get dressed, so she wore her night shirt with no bra, took no jacket, wore her sweatpants, and put on the military boots she brought, which ended up hurting her feet.

I think she did enjoy Assisi, but she whined for a lot of it. She had her own spending money and at one point wanted to buy a little dress she liked, but she had left her wallet in the room when she rushed out in the morning. She asked me for the money and told me it was my fault she left the wallet. She said it was because I was rushing her, but I refused to pay for it, so she went to Paul, and he lent her the money. She did end up paying him back.

M&M was still very upset that afternoon when we met up with Elise for lunch so Elise could interview her for her story, as she did with each of the homeless we took. M&M was still wearing her pajama shirt with no bra and her sweatpants. I remember being so frustrated with her, because I felt like that was so rude, but something Elise said afterward helped give me a little perspective. I hadn't really noticed it because I was still fuming, but at one point when Elise was asking M&M about her past and the judge wiping her record clean, M&M choked up a bit. Elise said M&M's whole voice and body language changed when she spoke about her record and what she had been charged with; she sounded sweeter, softer, and unsteady, like she was going to lose it and start crying at any minute because of how ashamed she was. When Elise told me that later, it really helped put things into perspective for me, and see M&M with different eyes.

She did apologize to me later, which I appreciated, and which took a lot on her part. Sometimes it's hard in the heat of difficult moments to remember just how big all of this is for the homeless we take, and that underneath all of that rebelliousness, M&M was still just a young girl who was overwhelmed and making major life changes. That was a reminder to myself too of how valuable it is to have other people's perspectives, because everyone perceives different things, and it can help to see the person in a different light, or in my case, with more patience!

When we did the Vatican tour, Paul was showing M&M around and since the two of them seemed fine, I said well, if you're going to be with M&M, I'm going with Raquel to the Sistine Chapel. He said he was okay with that, and we all agreed to meet outside at one of the fountains at a certain time. When I walked outside after the tour, I found M&M at one of the fountains all alone, crying, and some Italian people were trying to help her contact me because she thought she had been left behind. I was furious. I blasted Paul for allowing that to happen, because I trusted that he really would take care of her, but didn't. When I confronted him about it, he said he didn't feel it was his job. We had a big fight over that, and after that incident I didn't trust anyone. That was another teaching moment for me, because after all, it really wasn't their job to watch out for M&M, it was mine. I could only blame myself because I had chosen to take some free time to myself. The trips are not about me, and they are not for me: They are for the person we choose to take. That is the whole idea of these trips; it has been from the beginning — yet I so easily forget!

We also attended one of Pope Francis's general audiences that year with the *baciamano* tickets, so M&M was able to meet the pope. She had another meltdown while we were waiting for it to start, over some drama that happened in her past, and for a few minutes I thought I just might toss her off the platform. But eventually she calmed down and I think she actually really enjoyed meeting the pope. She said he was very sweet and kind, and she told him a bit about her father, who she said considers himself spiritual but not religious. The pope ended up giving her a blessing, and they also gave her a Rosary blessed by the pope that she said she was going to give to her father. I thought that was very thoughtful of M&M. Even though she's not religious herself, and even though she resented a lot of the "churchy" things we did on that trip, she didn't blow it off. She took advantage of the moment for herself and for a loved one.

We did have a lot of fun on that trip, despite the challenges. We did a Segway tour one day, and I was with M&M. She was great on her Segway, of course, and yes, I was very nervous — but I did it, even in the middle of bad Roman traffic! I believe M&M really did like the rest of the girls, and I know she enjoyed seeing the Trevi Fountain, which is always a favorite. It was a relaxing and informal time. On the plane ride home, she seemed to bond with the other young adults in the group. The tension was gone, and the laughter and storytelling continuous! A real camaraderie appeared to be going on, and despite the hiccups of group travel, in that moment I was happy other people were there for M&M to share with.

Having Your Eyes Opened by the Homeless

I've been in touch with M&M off and on since coming back, but we haven't been in consistent contact, and I don't think she's stayed in touch with any of the other people from the group, so what impact Rome had on her, I can't say. It's in God's hands, but I do know from talking with some of the girls in the young adult group that just being around a homeless person had an impact on their lives.

Mary Lakey, one of M&M's roommates in Rome, wrote me a while back about the trip from her perspective, and what she had to say captures so well the attitude of people who have no previous experience with the homeless. It is a very accurate summary of how so many people who are inexperienced or unfamiliar with street life tend to think, at least in my experience.

This is what Mary had to say:

I grew up in a very small, country town in rural Idaho and had never been around homeless people, so was totally unsure of what to expect traveling in a foreign country with M&M. Tanya told us about M&M before we met her. She warned me that she probably wouldn't be very nice to me and would probably say awful things to me. She also told me that M&M had been told she couldn't bring weapons. My very inexperienced self was honestly fairly frightened about what interacting with M&M might be like. I remember telling Tanya I was worried M&M would make me cry and Tanya told me she probably would. My first real memory of being around M&M was at a fundraising fish fry. She was so much smaller and more childish than I had expected. I immediately felt like she was a younger sister or high school cousin. The fundraiser was at a church, and I was slightly shocked by some of the things she said during the fundraiser, but ultimately was relieved that it had gone smoothly and she hadn't been mean to me!

The morning we left for Rome, Tanya picked me up first and then headed to the motel where M&M was staying to pick her up. Tanya told me not to get out of the car and that I shouldn't go inside with her. Again, I felt outside of my comfort zone and a little scared, totally unsure of what I was actually getting into. On the car ride she argued with one of the guys. I can't remember exactly about what, but it involved animals being hurt, I think. I remember feeling a little shocked by her opinions and realizing that we had very different belief systems. However, being around M&M at the airport just continued to make me feel maternal toward her. She was like a young kid, and I found myself making sure she was behaving. On the airplane, she was afraid of taking off at one point, so I let her hold my hand. This was the start of her and I having a bit more of a unique relationship than it seemed like she had with the other pilgrims. She seemed to be more on the friend level with them, but definitely more child/mother with me. She had no problem asking me for what she wanted, like to have my headphones or for food or drinks. I tried to make sure I drew a line where I was helping her out so as to not let her take advantage of me. I remember feeling like I was overthinking it though because in turn, she was the most generous person! She was always quick to offer anything she had to me or anyone else. That was a good lesson for me in giving what I have and not being so selfish.

While traveling, there were times she was being really negative, and I wished I could convince her what she was missing out on by having a bad attitude. There were also times she made fun of things the rest of us believed being at the Vatican. I never knew how to talk to her about that stuff, but I tried to just be open to her thoughts and offer my own. Sometimes she would open up and be very friendly and vulnerable and other times she would shut down completely. I remember her crying and certain exchanges between her and Tanya being tense. Sometimes I wondered what was really happening behind the scenes there. Usually at lunch or dinner when we had wine, there would be some awkward moments because she wasn't supposed to be drinking alcohol but clearly wanted to. Tanya got after her about what she was wearing sometimes too and told her she needed to be respectful of the guys in our group. I could tell Tanya wanted to make sure M&M stayed safe and in line. I generally tried to avoid being in the middle of those confrontations.

I shared a room with M&M and Raquel in Rome for a week. M&M's suitcase had a terrible odor that made our entire room smell. There were times it was nearly unbearable. She wasn't very comfortable bathing and that was noticeable. There were mornings that she wouldn't get out of bed at all or would be up late at night. One night she slept in the bathroom, and I couldn't figure out if Raquel and I had done something terrible to make her feel uncomfortable with us. Other nights she would talk to us as we were all falling asleep, and it would feel like any other girlfriend was in the room. Again, I just never knew which side of her we would get — the open, young side or the closed off, tough side.

When we returned to Denver, she lied to Tanya about where we should drop her off and we ended up having to wait for someone to get home or something like that. I was curious what the impact of going to Rome really had been for her.

Overall, I think being on the trip with M&M actually really helped me grow as a person. I couldn't tell how much she got from being around us, but I definitely learned a lot from her. As previously mentioned, I learned to be more generous and more open with my beliefs and to hearing about other people's. I left feeling grateful for my upbringing and support of loved ones after hearing her stories and things she had been through. I also left knowing that I needed to do a better job sharing love with people. I still wonder if her life was changed by the trip or if she knows that she helped change our lives.

Tanya going on this trip year after year is amazing. What an emotional journey to continue to take!

We All Have Choices

Sometime after coming back, M&M wrote a promotional blurb for the DHM website saying, "To take homeless youthful peeps outside of the country is an awesome opportunity to experience a part of the world most couldn't." She did complain about how strongly religion factored into her trip, but other than that her position was, "Take 'em out, it's a beautiful thing to see the world."

She did lie to me when we got back to Denver. She told me she was going to stay at a cousin's house so we drove her there and when we arrived, she took her luggage around back and left it there, but said no one was home and asked if I could just take her downtown and drop her off somewhere. By then I knew she had lied to me. Finally, she confessed and said that whoever's house it was said she could leave her luggage there. I said no, I can call someone to get you housing, or we can take you to the police station so you can get a voucher, but I made it clear I was not taking her back to the streets to be homeless. So, she called a couple of friends who came to pick her up and we waited over an hour for them to get there since it was rush-hour.

From that point, I had no contact with M&M until she messaged me from Seattle and asked if I would consider taking one of her friends on one of the Rome trips. I said I would definitely keep that in the back of my mind, and that was it. I do know that she eventually had a daughter, because after about a year, a friend of hers posted a picture of M&M with her little girl to Facebook, but I have not been in contact with her myself. It's certainly not for the lack of trying, but she is on her own path now, and I trust the Lord knows what he's doing!

I hope M&M will be able to break the cycle of her past. I don't know what's going on in her life now, and maybe I'll never know; but I do believe that God wanted her on that Rome trip for a reason. Maybe it had nothing to do with Rome. Maybe it was all about that moment in the courthouse before we even set off, when her whole slate was wiped clean. She didn't need all of that history, all of those charges, hanging over her reminding her of why she should be ashamed of herself. She received a great gift, and with all that gone, I hope she was able to start a new chapter in her life without falling into the same cycles that got her on the streets to begin with. M&M still has and always will have her own choices to make, but so do we all. That's what God's mercy is all about!

7

KATIE

We Are Called to a Full Life

In 2019, the sixth year we did the Rome trip, we took a young woman named Katie Henke, called "Twin" on the streets. This was another one of my favorite trips. It seems like the pattern the last few years was to have a difficult trip, then a great one, then another difficult one, and then a great one. Well, M&M's trip was definitely a challenge for me, but Katie's was a lot of fun. She still struggled a bit, and there were some ups and downs, but it was a lot better. I think that's in part because we went on our own again, so there was less pressure on her than if we had gone in a group setting again, but we still had a chaperone.

Life on the Streets

Just seven years prior to her trip in 2019, Katie never would never have imagined that one day she would be chosen. At that point, she was addicted to meth, struggling with mental illness, and drinking so heavily that she would get physically sick without hard liquor. She probably would have asked what drugs you were on if you told her that within a few years, she would be staring at Michelangelo's *Last Judgment* — a cornerstone of High Renaissance art — inside the Sistine Chapel, and his famous frescoes depicting scenes of God's creation of the world on the chapel's ceiling. Those are widely considered to be among the greatest artistic masterpieces of all time, and Katie never imagined she would get to see them.

At twenty-five, Katie had been through more than most: mental illness, the divorce of her parents, chronic depression, homelessness, drug and alcohol addiction, recovery, and motherhood. Katie's family has a long history of mental illness, and she herself began to experience chronic depression at age seven. After her parents split up and after a series of deaths in her family, Katie started to struggle a lot more, and her relationship with her mother became toxic. After a couple of failed suicide attempts, Katie's mother told her that if she wasn't happy, she could leave. And that's exactly what Katie did, ending up on the streets at fifteen.

Katie's father had been homeless at the time, and she had no other family to live with, so she was sleeping on the streets and was eventually befriended by some *juggalos* and *gutter punks*, meaning the street crowd, who watched out for her. In her own words, Katie once said she left home because "I couldn't stand it there anymore," referring to her mother. She said she felt "more at home sleeping on the concrete sidewalks with these people than I did at my own house." Her street friends helped her find food and provided her with protection. Soon after ending up on the streets, Katie started squatting with a woman near the Platte River who called her "Twin," because the woman swore Katie looked exactly like her own daughter, who was around Katie's age. The name stuck.

Soon she started drinking and within a year had become an alcoholic, drinking hard liquor every day. Once she realized she was an addict, and that she was getting physically sick without booze, she was able to kick the habit. But by then she had started to use methamphetamines too, which she found much harder to quit. She had become stuck in a cycle she couldn't get out of: depression, getting high, and stealing to feed her habit. At times she would sit in her makeshift camp for days when her depression flared up, without eating, or sleeping, or even going to the bathroom unless it was an absolute necessity. In these moments, just being in public seemed to physically hurt, and meth helped her to escape for a while. Though she only smoked it for two years, to this day she insists that the amount she consumed in that time should have killed her.

For Katie, the breaking point came in 2012, when she was eighteen and found out she was pregnant. Despite her intense fears about pregnancy and motherhood, something inside told her she needed that baby. Though she still struggles with depression, ever since her daughter was born, she swears that the bad days when she either couldn't or didn't want to move are gone. Shortly before her daughter's birth, Katie's mother let her move back in so she could get on her feet and raise the baby. Despite their history, they made it work, and Katie was able to be at home with her daughter for the first few years after she was born. She stayed with her mother until 2018, when her mother asked them to move out. So, Katie got a job at a place called Purple Door Coffee, a specialty espresso bar and coffee roaster in Denver that employs teens and young adults who have been homeless and want to get off the streets. It is run by a ministry called Dry Bones, whose name is taken from Ezekiel 37: "Behold, I will cause breath to enter you, and you shall live. And I will lay sinews upon you, and will cause flesh to come upon you, and cover you with skin, and put breath in you, and you shall live" (vv. 5–6).

Each homeless person hired there must present a resume that Dry Bones missionaries will help to compile, and each candidate must go through the interview process before getting the position. Once hired, the new employee is required to dress appropriately and come to work on time for their shift. Despite her fears that she would somehow mess up and lose the job, Katie stayed on and was finally able to get an apartment for her and her daughter, which was the biggest and scariest step she has taken in her adult life.

Meeting Katie on the streets and watching how her life changed when her daughter was born was so inspiring. Whenever I stopped in at Purple Door and saw Katie make and serve coffee, I was proud. And I was so happy when she finally got her own apartment, knowing how stressful it was and how much anxiety she had about holding down a job, trying to be there for her daughter, and still struggling with bouts of depression.

Months before taking Katie to Rome, as I was clocking in hours of fundraising, I was surprised and very moved one day when I got this message from Katie's father. In it, he said: "This is my daughter Katie. I don't say it enough, but I am very proud of what she has accomplished, and to all of you that have given to the fund to get her to Rome, I want to thank everyone for making this possible." To me this was a wonderful sign of the healing process. While Katie was on the Rome trip, Katie's mother kept her daughter, and her dad picked her up from school. It's amazing how children seem to have a way of healing many past hurts.

When it came to choosing the person to go to Rome in 2019, it was the same process: I prayed about it, and God put Katie in my path. I got the gut-level feeling I always do when I'm trying to decide who should go to Rome after I walked into the Purple Door Coffee shop one day and saw Katie working. As soon as I saw her, in that instant, I felt it, and from that moment I knew that Katie was the person who was supposed to go. From there, everything fell into place.

When I asked Katie if she wanted to go to Rome, she was both overwhelmed and completely overjoyed, and also "shocked" that she had been selected. She had known about the program and always wanted to go, but never thought it would happen to her. During the fundraising process, Katie said she believed the trip would make "a huge positive impact in my life in ways I might not even know are possible yet." She was right.

Rome-ward Bound

When I first met Katie on the streets, she was standoffish and "hardcore," but you'd never know that seeing the sweet, open, and vulnerable young woman that she turned into as soon as we set foot in Rome. There wasn't a lot of prep work to do for her, because she didn't have a record, so getting her passport and wardrobe set was a cinch compared to past trips.

On the day we left for Rome, Katie and our chaperones Meredith Maxwell, Raquel Mora, and myself got to the airport four hours early to be sure we had plenty of time to get checked in, go through security and find our gate, and do it all at our own pace, as this was really the first time that Katie had ever traveled. She was scared, excited, and anxious all at once. Not only was it a ten-hour plane ride, but it was also the first time she had left her daughter for so long. Both her daughter and Katie's father came with her to the airport to say goodbye. Katie was emotional and extremely anxious, but after getting through security and having something to eat, her nerves calmed a bit, and she was ready to board the plane for our layover in Frankfurt.

When we got there, there was some confusion about boarding times, so we missed our connecting flight to Rome, and were forced to take a later flight. We ended up arriving in Rome around midnight, so when we got to our hotel, we couldn't do anything except collapse on our pillows and go to sleep! But despite the late night, we were up early for Mass the next morning at St. Anthony Abbot at the Esquiline, a Russian Greek Catholic Church. It was a two-hour Mass, and Katie honestly made it through more of it than I expected, but she did have to step out for a smoke and ended up just waiting for us outside.

Right after Mass on that first day, we visited the ancient Basilica of St. Clement, saw the Colosseum, the Pantheon, a famous espresso bar in Rome called San Eustachio, and spent time just wandering the streets. I was amazed at what a trooper Katie was right from the beginning. Not only did she handle the Mass situation better than I expected, but she was also very interested and curious during our visits to the other monuments we saw. She was constantly asking questions, which surprised me, because I thought she would find all the historical stuff boring, but she was genuinely interested and really took time to look at everything we saw.

Small Miracles

Eventually we ended up at the Trevi fountain, which is a favorite stop for each of the people we've taken. It is traditional for us on these trips to do the Trevi fountain "coin toss." It has long been an urban legend in Rome that if a visitor tosses a coin over their back and makes it into the fountain, they will come back one day. In 2005 the City of Rome, which collects the coins every night, decided to donate the funds collected from the Trevi to the Rome branch of a Catholic charity organization called Caritas International, because of all the work they do with city's poor.

I think it was that first night at the Trevi that it all really began to hit Katie for the first time. She kept staring at the fountain; she was so absorbed by it that it seemed to be some sort of a spiritual release for her. I think it was finally sinking in that she had actually made it, and that she could just enjoy the beauty of the experience without worrying about all the stuff she had to back home. I remember that at one point, as she looked at the fountain, her eyes filled with tears, and she could not stop thanking me for bringing her. I couldn't help myself, and I started tearing up too. I felt like my heart could burst at any minute. It was a special moment for us, and I believe it was a life-changing moment for Katie. It really set the tone for the rest of the trip. Katie ended up tossing several coins into the fountain before deciding she was finally ready for dinner, though I don't know how any of us had room, because we had eaten so much gelato!

We went to Assisi that year too and Katie really liked the city, but what she liked more than anything was the food! For lunch, we had a lasagna made with a cream sauce and broccoli, which is common in Italy but not so much in the United States. Katie liked it so much that she still talks about it to this day. She talked about it so much when we got back, that the girls who went the year after specifically requested that we stop at the same restaurant in Assisi so they could try it too.

There was no real "turning point" for Katie in this trip. For her, the entire week, especially since that first night at the Trevi, was one big moment of grace. It was like she was in some altered state — she was in constant awe, and she was happier than I had ever seen her. Of course, there were moments of frustration along the way, and there were times when she needed to go have a smoke to keep her cool. She had a hard time with the big crowds and people bustling around way too close, and there were a few other things that bothered her along the way, but Katie always kept a level head, and to me, that spoke volumes.

I think Katie experienced several miracles during this trip;

not anything big, but the small kind you don't really see at the time, but which have a special inspiration in the moment that changes something in you and sets you off on a different course. Most of these moments actually came from our visit to the Vatican, which is surprising because Katie wasn't a practicing believer.

During the second half of the week, we visited St. Peter's Basilica and the Vatican Museums, and we attended one of Pope Francis's general audiences. The day we visited the basilica started out with a Scavi tour, which takes visitors underneath St. Peter's Basilica to see small chapels filled with frescoes and signatures of soldiers who fought in the Second World War. It ends by taking visitors to a space under the main altar of the basilica where what are believed to be the bones of Saint Peter himself are buried. When the tour ends, the group exits directly into the basilica, which we hadn't seen yet, and it took Katie's breath away as she came up the stairs and caught her first glimpse of the inside. She kept staring at the marble floors, the statues, and the golden Holy Spirit window behind the main altar. I think she felt like a VIP coming in through that entrance, instead of waiting in the long line out front. For those who have experienced things like riding business class on an airplane, an exclusive private tour of something important, or even front row seats at a concert, something as simple as coming out into the basilica after a tour versus waiting in a long line might not seem like much. But for someone whose entire life has conditioned them to believe that they are worthless and undeserving of unique opportunities, a special moment can be a life-changer.

Yet what I think actually had the biggest impact on Katie that day came later. After looking around inside the basilica, we went to lunch and then came back to visit the Vatican Museums and the Sistine Chapel. That is where Katie had what I would describe as an "eye-opening life change." Like every other tourist, we weaved our way through the Museums, which were always packed like a can of sardines — at least in the pre-COVID era — and we ended up in the Sistine Chapel. I told this story in the introduction, but it's worth telling again here.

As we were standing there looking around inside the Sistine Chapel, a priest who sat in a chair beside the main altar stood up every few minutes to tell everyone to keep their voices down. Raquel and I felt very moved being there, so we went up to the priest to ask if we could go to confession while we were there. I went first, and then Raquel, and Katie sat and waited. But as Raquel was standing up to go, Katie asked if she was allowed to go too, since she wasn't a practicing Catholic. Raquel told her it was fine and to go get in line if she wanted to. And to my surprise, Katie did. I was shocked because Katie was never really that religious. It was a very courageous step for anyone in her position, far from home and her friends and family, and especially given her anxiety, but she did it.

She and the priest spoke for a while, and when Katie came back, she had tears in her eyes. I wasn't sure what happened, but when we asked if she was okay, Katie said she had been thinking about her daughter, and that she told the priest some of her background and said she didn't think she had been a good mother. I think she was expecting to be reprimanded, but instead the priest told her that she was a good mother, and not to be so hard on herself; that she was doing her best, that she loved her daughter, and needed to give herself a break. When Katie told us this, I think we all started crying! I think that was probably one of the most important moments of the trip, because despite the fear and discomfort she probably felt just by going up there, Katie got some much-needed reassurance about the most important thing in her life, and she left the chapel holding her head a little higher.

The next morning, we went to Pope Francis's general audience, and this year Katie and I had the special front-row *baci-*

amano tickets again. I didn't know this at the time, but Katie's experience there led to a small miracle in my own life and faith. Despite getting up extremely early to get to our seats and the hours-long wait for the pope to get there, Katie still said it was a highlight. At the time, I remember her saying, "It was just so surreal. Getting to do something that you never thought you'd get to do in your lifetime is just shocking at first. It was amazing to get to hold his hand in mine even for a moment. It was definitely an honor."

That statement later had a totally unexpected impact on me and my own relationship with the Eucharist, which Catholics believe is the true Body and Blood of Jesus Christ. After returning home from that trip, I attended a Mass at my parish and as I was walking up to receive Communion, that statement from Katie popped into my mind, and I began to weep as the consecrated Host was placed in my hand. If Katie felt so moved just touching the pope, what should I feel holding Jesus himself in my hands? It brought tears to my eyes, and I didn't want to let go. I felt like he was holding my hand. Now every time I go to the Roman Catholic Church and receive Jesus in my hands (I normally go to a Byzantine church, and they do Communion differently), I am so excited to be able to hold him just for a moment. This means the world to me. Katie's statement brought the Eucharist to life for me, and that is a little miracle I will always be grateful for.

Experiences like this have convinced me, and others who have been a part of the trips, that the visit to Rome is not just a teaching experience for the homeless individuals who go, but also for us. They are the ones who teach me!

Throughout the trip, Katie would scour the ground looking for coins so she could save them up and light candles for her friends and loved ones inside the churches we went into. She lit so many candles, I wondered whether there would be any left for other visitors! Katie would often get emotional when talking about the people she loved, both family and friends on the streets, and how badly she wanted them to experience the same things she was. One person she specifically lit a candle for and could not stop talking about was Binky, the young woman who took her own life and whose death almost made me quit doing homeless ministry altogether. The funny thing is, and I did not know at the time this is how things would work out, Katie kept talking about Binky during the trip. The next year, in 2020, it was Binky's little sister Angelique who would be selected for the Rome trip. I truly believe this was an act of the Holy Spirit, as I did not plan this myself.

From that moment with Pope Francis, the rest of the trip seemed to speed by. One of our favorite stops was the "bone church," which is actually called Santa Maria della Concezione dei Cappuccini and is run by the Capuchin Franciscan order. It has a small underground crypt containing the skeletal remains of some three thousand seven hundred Capuchin friars buried by the order and displayed on the walls in ornate designs and even lanterns. Part of the original reason for arranging the bones this way was because at the time, so many friars were dying from the Black Plague that the Capuchins had run out of space to bury them underground, so they found creative uses for their bones above ground. To this day the Capuchins insist that the display is not anything morbid but is rather a reminder of the *momento mori* and one's own mortality.

We spent our last day in Italy on a day trip to Venice, walking around the city taking pictures, shopping, and eating gelato like any other tourist. In hindsight, a trip to Venice was a bit much, and I likely will not try to squeeze it into future trips, but it was still a highlight for us. Even though we had somehow got ourselves up for a 5:30 a.m. train ride that day, and did not get back to Rome until after ten o'clock at night, we spent our last night at a gelato shop across from the Airbnb apartment where we were staying. We were exhausted, but we had so much fun!

At the end of the trip, before we went back, Katie said her dream was to get a job that allowed her more flexibility and to save up money so that one day she can come back to Rome with her mother, who has never traveled but loves art. They still have a complicated relationship, but it's a process they are taking step-by-step. The love is there, which is the most important thing, and this comment from Katie showed me just how much she wants that relationship to change for the better.

Coming Back Different

Not long after we got back from Italy, Katie wrote me a personal note reiterating her thanks both to me personally, and to DHM for offering her the chance to go:

> It's been about a week and a half since I got back from Italy, I'm sorry it took so long but I just wanted to give a huge THANK YOU to the Denver Homeless Ministry for giving me the once in a lifetime opportunity that they did! I got to see the Trevi fountain, eat REAL gelato (so amazing!), I got to see the hills of Assisi and even pet some kitties while I was there! I got to eat some of the most delicious foods, experience the beauty of the bone church, walk alongside the rivers of Venice, and built some amazing memories with an old friend and gained new ones! I love you girls! [Raquel Mora & Meredith Maxwell, chaperones] Thank you so much for the time spent and the love shown! Thank you again Denver Homeless Ministry for everything you guys do! You change lives!

That last line of Katie's note, the part where she says we change lives, expressed so well what we hope and pray is the end result of each of the trips we lead!

Those who go to Rome do not come back the same. Whether the change is big or small, immediate or in the future, the seeds have been planted, and I trust that the Lord will help them grow. I have always been an adamant opponent of proselytism, so I refuse to preach to the people I take, nor do I force them to go inside churches, attend Masses, or make acts of reverence they do not mean or wish to make. Everything they do has to be up to them; it has to be their own choice. I try my best to love them, despite my own shortcomings — which, if I'm being honest, are not something I want to count, especially my hard-headed impatience! — and I try to help them see the good in themselves and to recognize and value themselves for who they are, not for who they were or what they've done.

Like many others who have gone to Rome, when Katie first found out she was going, she asked herself, "Why me? I'm not worthy of going, why did you choose me?" Though the road is far from over, Katie's perception of herself is already starting to change, and from what I've heard from those close to her, she's starting to see a little more beauty in herself every day. Instead of simply spending many of her days depressed, she has finally accepted that she needs help. She sought out a psychiatrist and was formally diagnosed with Bipolar and is now receiving medication and counseling. Though she might not always feel like it, she has made significant strides and her whole attitude has changed. It's remarkable.

I truly believe that Rome gave Katie both the desire and the motivation to start seeking help. Suddenly life wasn't so dreary, and I think she saw just how happy and fun life can be. I don't think her heart had ever been that full, and once a person experiences that, they want more, and they'll fight to get to it. Katie has always been a fighter, mostly for her daughter, but now for herself too. Even though Katie didn't feel worthy of being chosen,

I told her the same thing I have consistently told each person: I did not choose you, God chose you. He sees something in you that is worthy. My job is to help *you* see it!

8

ANGELIQUE

We All Need Family

When I chose Angelique Vargas, Binky's little sister, for our trip to Rome in 2020, the decision was totally unexpected. As usual, I was praying about who the Lord wanted me to take after we got back from our trip with Katie. In the process, I actually did something I've never done before, and I asked Katie who she thought would be the perfect person to go, because I wasn't getting that clear gut feeling about anyone that I normally do. Well, Katie suggested I take Angelique, because it was the tenth anniversary of Binky's suicide. When she said that, my heart did a flip-flop and I knew beyond a shadow of a doubt she was the one that should go!

Losing a Sister

Angelique, who prefers to go by "Duckie" on the street, had always been close to her older sister. Their family had six siblings, but Angelique only grew up around her sister Binky and their brother Christopher. Both of their parents were addicted to drugs and weren't around a lot, so the kids spent a lot of time on their own. When they were young, their parents split and they lived with their father, who ended up marrying another woman who was extremely abusive. Binky, as the older sister, was always very protective of Angelique, and tried to shield her as much as possible from their stepmother's abuse. Angelique always said Binky was like a mother to her, and she was closer to Binky than any of her other siblings. Eventually their mom got custody of the kids again, but because of all her problems, she never really kept track of the kids and Binky and Angelique ended up leaving for periods at a time to live on the streets. Sometimes things at home were so bad that Binky would take Angelique out during the day and would teach her the "street smarts" and survival tactics she would need to make it out there. I truly think Binky was the only person who really made Angelique feel loved, so when Binky killed herself in 2010, it shook Angelique to the core, and I don't think she ever recovered, not really.

After Binky's suicide, Angelique started having problems of her own. Her relationship with her mother disintegrated, and at age fifteen she started running away. She lived with her grandparents for around five months until she got into trouble and was sent back to stay with her mother. When her mother found out she had caused trouble with her grandparents, she was furious and didn't want Angelique to come back into the house, so Angelique started living on the streets. She was a bum for the entire winter that year, and to this day she'll tell you that one of the biggest lessons she learned was, "Do not trust every nice person. Some people out there want to hurt you in any way they can, and you just can't trust them." Angelique was very hurt and confused at that point, and so she took off and started traveling for a year. She ended up visiting ten states, rail-riding and hitchhiking to get around. While she would still describe it as one of the best years of her life, she knew she had to come home and set things straight, so she came back to Denver and ended up moving back in with her mom. She was still kicked out a few times, but I think she and her mom both knew deep down that there was just no more room for heartache and pain in their lives, so Angelique was always let back in.

They still live together to this day. It's not easy, and they still have problems to deal with, but Angelique from the beginning was determined to make her best effort every day to make things work, because she wants to be better than her past experiences. I know there are many times when she's wanted to call it quits, but she's making the effort, and that speaks volumes.

A Friend Comes Along

Angelique was the youngest person we'd ever taken — she was only eighteen when she went to Rome in 2020. But that year for the first time we were joined by another young woman, Cassi McPhail, who was twenty-seven and used to be homeless, but by then was making ends meet and was able to pay her own way to Rome.

Cassi had spent most of her adolescent life on the streets due to family problems at home, so she was familiar with the street crowd and considered many of them friends. As she got older, she would sometimes sleep in her car for months at a time when she couldn't afford to pay rent. She got her first job when she was nineteen, and that helped change the course of her life. She ended up going back to school and eventually joined a medical assistance program. At the time of the trip, she was working at a family practice and was also working a second retail job so she could pay the bills. Cassi had known about the Rome trips and had always wanted to go, so she asked if she could tag along.

Since she hadn't been chosen to go, Cassi knew she would have to pay her own way and was prepared to do that. I still had not heard from her by the time we purchased our plane tickets, because she was working a lot, but when she realized that she had missed the deadline, she messaged me right away and said that she really wanted to go still. I told her that I needed the money for the plane trip ASAP, and I was able to find a flight for the same price as ours leaving and arriving at the same time as ours. So, I booked her on that once she sent me her passport information, which she also got at the last minute, but she managed to get it done. Then before the trip, amazingly, she paid the money that was required in full. That surprised me, as I had not expected her to pull it off, so I knew she was meant to go.

Throughout the planning process, Cassi was easier to stay in touch with, and she was more open and willing to discuss what she needed and was extremely excited about the chance to go. I personally bought her luggage and had it delivered to her house. And Cassi is the one that got herself and Angelique to the airport. Not many people would have come through the way she did, especially at the last minute. I've always admired Cassi's strength and determination. Her path hasn't been easy, as is the case for so many youth who end up on the streets, but I'm confident she will succeed, despite the ups and downs along the way, and that is in large part thanks to these qualities.

I was already living in Missouri by the time I asked Angelique to go. I had moved back to be closer to family, so I wasn't there to handle everything in person like I usually did. I know Angelique was living with her mother still when I popped the question, but I don't know much more than that, as I wasn't around anymore. I believe she still hung out with her street friends on a regular basis. Whether she still slept on the streets at times, I don't know.

Prior to the trip, I was constantly in touch with Angelique to make sure she had everything she needed, since I wasn't there physically to help her get everything in order. A friend of mine named Maureen from Stand Up for Kids chipped in and made sure that Angelique got her luggage, which she picked out from Amazon and had delivered to her, as well as phone adapters and spending money. Since Angelique never graduated high school, Maureen really wanted her to get her GED, so she talked to another friend who got Angelique bus passes so she could go back and forth to school. Well, that didn't go over well. Angelique ended up getting very upset about Maureen asking her why she hadn't applied to school yet, so she cut all ties with Maureen later on. I agreed with Maureen that Angelique should get her GED, but I backed off, although I still wish she would get it. The woman who donated the bus tickets said they were for a specific reason and refused to pay for any more of them. I do not believe that Angelique has taken further steps to get her GED at this point, and I do not believe that she has done anything to better herself in that manner.

Taking Chances

The COVID-19 coronavirus broke out as preparations were underway. At first, no one thought much of it, because it seemed limited to Asia for the most part, however, before too long reports came out saying that it had reached Europe, and Italy was the hotspot. Most of the infections were up north, farther away from Rome, but they were starting to record a lot of cases, and things seemed to change every day. There was a constant back-and-forth about whether we should or shouldn't go, because it seemed like a lockdown might happen, but everything was still open when we purchased our tickets.

Of all of us, Angelique had the most anxiety about the trip. She was nervous, but afraid she would never get another chance to go. That year, Raquel was supposed to join us again as a chaperone, and at one point Angelique talked to her and Cassi and said she had decided to go ahead and go, because she didn't know when another opportunity would come along. I was happy to hear that, but I made sure everyone was on the same page, because they did not have to go if they didn't want to. I could not guarantee that there would be another trip, but Raquel and Cassi were adamant that they wanted to go, so when Angelique said she had decided she wanted to go too, it was on, even knowing what could possibly happen. None of us realized then what would actually happen, but we were ready for the adventure.

Chasing the Lockdown

Given the circumstances, this trip was probably the most unique from day one. Unfortunately, Raquel was not able to go, because I misspelled her name when I made the plane reservations, so she was refused boarding at the airport because her documents did not match her ticket, which I felt awful about. We spent two hours trying to get it fixed, but the airline insisted they could not change the name for an international flight, so we had to leave her behind. It was very disappointing, first of all because of all the planning and excitement, but also because this meant that we didn't have a second chaperone, which I always insist on for these trips. Raquel tried to get it fixed when she got back home, but they still refused to change it, and in the end, I had to bite the bullet and pay her back $1500 since she had paid her own way. That was a very hard lesson for me to learn considering I had insisted that this was supposedly going to be the last Rome trip. The only trouble with that is, I say something like that every trip I take, and always seem to end up doing another one. I'm not sure when the Lord will let me retire, but until then, I keep learning lessons, usually the hard way!

That was the first of many hiccups on this trip. It was truly an adventure from beginning to end. As it turns out, we got to Rome just when lockdowns in Italy started to happen. We ended up having only two days in Rome and one in Assisi before we had to make a quick escape to avoid getting stuck.

The trip happened in March, and almost as soon as we arrived, things started shutting down. We got to do some stuff the first day or two that we were there, but it seemed like every night we would look at our itinerary, and by the next morning whatever we had planned on doing that day had been shut down. I had no idea what to do. We did get to see Assisi, which the girls loved, but with museums, monuments, and even bars and restaurants closing when we were in Rome, we ended up just walking around outside the places that were closed, such as the Colosseum and the Pantheon, talking about the history of the place and what happened there. Since I had been to Rome and seen all of these places before, I was able to give some background, which the girls appreciated. When we visited the Pantheon, there was a little crack in the door, so we each took turns peeking inside, which was fun. We also stopped by the Trevi, as we do on every trip, but by then it had been roped off and was being guarded by police, as no one was allowed to go down because they were afraid of crowds. That was disappointing, because it's a favorite spot and by then tossing a coin into the fountain had become a tradition, but it was also fascinating for us to see how Rome was closing down. Little did I know that only a few weeks later we would be going through the same thing in the United States!

A couple coffee shops were still open when we were there, so we got lots of coffee and gelatos. One day we stopped to eat lunch at a restaurant near the Pantheon that was open and still had indoor and outdoor seating. We chose to eat inside because it was a little chilly that day, but we wanted to sit by the window, so they seated us at a table for three overlooking the few pedestrians that were out and a couple of people that were sitting at tables. Before our food actually arrived, the police came into the building and said something in Italian to the owner, who then came to our table and told us we would have to separate as we were sitting too close together. At the time, people were required to be at least three feet apart, so they brought another table in and put one of us at the end of that table. The owner was very embarrassed about that, so he brought us dessert for free. That was an experience we kept talking about, not necessarily because it was bad, but it was just something we weren't expecting. It's weird now to think that so soon after the trip, this became the norm almost all over the world, but we were at the heart of the pandemic in Europe at the time and were witnessing firsthand how things were being handled. Looking back, it all seems sort of surreal.

We were also supposed to meet Pope Francis at one of his general audiences during this trip. I had the special *baciamano* tickets again for Angelique and I to meet the pope, but of course all public papal audiences were suspended the week we arrived, so we only found out a few days in advance that we would not, in fact, be meeting the pope after all, and they wouldn't see St. Peter's Basilica or the Vatican Museums either, because it had all been closed off. All of this was of course disappointing, because the girls had been looking forward to seeing everything that the people who had gone on previous trips talked about, but they weren't devastated. Despite not being able to do most of this stuff, the girls themselves were amazing, and took it like champs. They had no meltdowns about this and handled everything very well.

Angelique did have some meltdowns of her own during the trip, but not that many. One day she had a major meltdown and started yelling at me in the middle of the street, criticizing me for anything I may or may not have done in a positive way toward her since we'd arrived. She apologized later when we were at dinner with Elise and her husband John, who cooked us *penne alla vodka* and let us eat and drink on their fabulous terrace. Some of the things Angelique said I owned and took to heart, and some things I just knew in my heart had nothing to do with me but were just part of her meltdown.

Most of Angelique's meltdowns came on March 9, the tenth anniversary exactly of her sisters' suicide. Anybody would be devastated, and emotional, to remember that day. Angelique was very young when that happened, so I am sure it was hard to understand, and Angelique had brought small vials of her sister's ashes to spread around the places we went, which she carried around with her, and I'm sure could not have been easy to do that day. She did sprinkle some of Binky's ashes in the different places we went, which might seem morbid, but it was important to her and since this trip was for her, I wasn't going to be the one to tell her no. I'm sure doing this was also very illegal, but we never got caught!

Enjoying Each Other's Company

Angelique and Cassi really bonded on this trip. They had no problem going outside of our apartment at night and asking the police for a cigarette or asking if they knew where they could buy a bottle of wine. The police were very polite and very helpful, and I think the girls thrived on that. Since there was really nothing else to do and there was no cable in our apartment, they spent their evenings during lockdown talking and drinking wine while I slept. We also all kind of bonded over the awkwardness of our living situation that week, because the apartment manager's son had a way of unlocking the door so he could come and go as he chose. In the mornings, we would find him sitting at the table with coffee ready for us when we got up in the morning, which we found slightly creepy, but tried to be polite about. Another lesson learned there — make sure we have our privacy and that no one else has access to the place when we're staying in it!

Since most of the stuff on our regular itinerary was not an option for this trip, we ended up finding other quirky things to do. One of our favorites was an adult-only Haunted Rome Ghost Tour. This gave us so many insights into Rome that we would never have known. It started at Castel Sant'Angelo, which is close to St. Peter's, and there was so much history about that place — gruesome history, but fascinating. We learned about the so-called "Witch of Rome" who helped over six hundred women kill their husbands by putting two drops of a specific poison into a glass of water a day, and was only caught because one woman poured the entire bottle in her husband's water by accident. It was funky, but interesting, and a part of history that most people would never have known.

After that, everything else shut down. On that trip more than any other, we learned to just "be" and to sit and enjoy each other's company. We laughed a lot, and since we were just flying by the seat of our pants and doing things based on whatever the situation was when we woke up — almost every day something new shut down or there was a new rule for COVID — it was more relaxed, and there was less pressure to stick to a schedule. The girls were amazing and didn't want to leave — they would have been OK with a thirty-day lock down if they got stuck! Even when the Italians started making us wear gloves and social distance inside grocery stores, the girls made it a fun experience. We bought a lot of food and wine to have a last meal in the apartment, because Angelique promised to cook dinner for Elise and John as a thank you for the dinner they made us. But because of the pandemic, we had to leave early and left all our food and wine for the landlady's son.

Racing against the Clock
We had only been in Rome for a couple of days when it became

clear that Italy was going into a full national lockdown, and we heard on the news that President Trump was going to close off all international flights by Friday at midnight. Our flight was scheduled to leave Rome Friday morning with a stop in Frankfurt, and we were supposed to arrive in Denver long before the cut off, but with travel to and from Italy pretty much coming to a halt that week, the airline canceled our flight. When they rescheduled us, there was a mistake with the timing for Frankfurt, meaning we would arrive after Trump's cutoff. I did not catch it, but my sister who was in Cape Girardeau caught the mistake and called me at 2:00 a.m. on Thursday morning, which was still Thursday night in the States, and asked what we were going to do. I had no idea what to do, so I wrote Elise and asked what she thought was the best course of action. She was confident that we would be able to get back in the United States no matter what since we are American citizens, but since things were so up in the air and seemed to be changing minute-to-minute, she said the best plan if we didn't want to get stuck was to forget whatever plans we had that night and pack up right away and head straight to the airport. As soon as she said that, it was off to the races!

I have to admit, when she said this, I slightly panicked, and went into the bedroom where the girls were sound asleep and told them they needed to get up right that second — no breakfast, no coffee, nothing — that we would get it at the airport, but we needed to pack our bags and go. Well, this kind of freaked them out a little bit, and I can understand why. But I'm glad I did that, because when we got to the taxi stand and grabbed a cab, our driver herded us into the car and said the police were going to shut down the taxi service. We were all holding our luggage on our laps, but we were happy we did that, because we were pretty much one of the last groups of people to get to the airport from Rome. I'm sure John and Elise would have let us crash at their place, but not indefinitely, and I certainly didn't want to take our chances!

When we got to the airport, we were told our flight was not until the next day, so I asked the woman at the desk to double check our reservation. She called someone else over to look at it, and they both confirmed we need to go on the flight to Frankfurt that was leaving then, so she took our luggage and said we had to pick it up in Frankfurt as we had an overnight stay and wouldn't get out of Frankfurt until the next morning. So, we were one of the last to board the flight to Frankfurt, and when we arrived, we looked for hotels close to the airport so there was no chance of missing our flight to Denver the next morning. As stressful as that morning was, it ended up being a fun night. We went to our hotel and got settled, and then walked around the streets a bit before going back to our hotel where we ate a traditional German dinner of brats and fries, which we of course washed down with some German beer. I think we all needed that beer after the whirlwind of the morning and almost getting stuck abroad, but we still had one more leg of the journey to make.

We got to the airport early the next morning because I was not going to take any chances, and it turns out it was a good thing we did that. When they went to print out Angelique's boarding pass they printed out Raquel's instead, so we needed to go back to customer service in Frankfurt and get it corrected before we could board the plane. But we managed to do that in time and boarded our plane just fine. When the plane took off, it was one of the best feelings in the world. I have friends who work at the Denver International Airport who did not think we were going to make it in time and were very surprised to see us come out of the international concourse.

After returning home, we were required to self-quarantine for fourteen days. At that time there were no COVID tests available, and since Cassi could not go back to her own apartment because there was a risk of potentially infecting her roommates, Angelique's mom allowed Cassi to stay with them for those days. I was in lockdown in my own house, so food and toilet paper were brought to my back porch for me to pick up. I worked at the local school at the time, and they agreed I should not come back until my fourteen days were up. Well, when my time was up, Cape Girardeau decided to implement its own quarantine, meaning I was in the house for another fourteen days. It was a weird end to a weird trip!

Nothing Is a Waste

Some people might be tempted to ask if this trip was all just a waste, since everything shut down and we weren't able to do most of the cool things we planned on, but I do not feel that this trip was wasted at all. It was an adventure, one I'm sure I never want to repeat, but still, it was interesting, fun in its own way, and Angelique and Cassi had a great time in spite of everything.

I do not know what the Lord's plans are for Angelique, or what his reasons were in selecting her for this trip. Clearly, this one was not about any of the sights and sounds, but it was about something else. What that is, I don't know, but God had a reason, and time will tell what impact this had on Angelique. Just getting to be there made a difference for her, I think, especially because she was there for the anniversary of Binky's suicide. It was almost as if making it there meant she had already overcome her past. Angelique still has a long way to go, for sure. She was young when she went, and she was so young when her sister died, that I don't think she ever really had the chance to grow up emotionally. She's been through a lot, but she has a big heart. She can have a strong will when she wants to, but she has a lot of growing to do still, and I think Rome helped push her forward a bit on that path.

Like many before her, I believe Angelique expected more from me than I could or wanted to give when we were in Rome. This left a bit of an emotional hole in both of us, yet time and the Lord heal, and I believe we are in this process.

Angelique is willing to fight for what she believes is right, and I've seen this part of her when it comes to overcoming her own past. Angelique is determined not to let past experiences of pain and suffering define her; she wants to be better than that, someone new who can offer a real contribution of good to the world. I truly believe she is on the right path, and that Rome somehow reinforced her on this part of her journey.

We have not stayed in regular contact, so I am not sure what Angelique is doing now. The last I knew she was still living with her mother, but I also know she has had to pay some bills, so it's possible she has a place of her own, but she hasn't been forthcoming with that information in our limited conversations. We text every now and then, but I never push her for information, and she rarely offers it. While her circumstances might not have changed, I do believe she has a story to tell and an experience she'll never forget from the lockdown in Rome and the quarantine!

In the Gospel of Matthew, one of the Beatitudes given by Jesus is "Blessed are the merciful, for they shall obtain mercy" (5:7). This is also relevant for Angelique, because she still needs to learn how to forgive, especially her mother. There is a lot of history there, a lot of pain to work through, and a lot to forgive. Angelique had an abusive childhood where her parents weren't around, and she has struggled to trust her family and stay off the streets. But her trip to Rome has helped in this process somehow, and it has motivated her to move forward and help other homeless youth.

We finally took another trip to Rome in 2022, a group trip with an older woman named Patti; Cassi was able to come too, because she had missed out on so much during this first trip. I had hoped that Angelique would be able to join us for that one too, since she also missed out on seeing so many things, but she wasn't able to make it. I was disappointed, but I know it's all in God's hands, and if he wants her to come back, it will happen. If not, then I trust he has his reasons and if I've learned anything by now, it's not to get in the way! The trip we took with Angelique in 2020 was meant to be, and may not show results right away, but I am sure that there will be results and they will be positive. I may not see what the Lord sees until after the fact, but he has *never* disappointed. Angelique has told me before that she wants these trips to continue so bad that she's willing to try to do them herself!

No matter what her path is going forward, I know that Angelique is going to blossom like a butterfly. Not only has her life been impacted by her experiences in Rome, but I am confident that she will change the way people around her view the world!

9
THE STORY ISN'T OVER

Finding God in the Unexpected

The last trip I took with the DHM wasn't anything like I'd planned. So often, God seems to have a funny way of taking my plans and turning them upside down or veering off in a direction I absolutely did not see or intend. Our last trip to Rome was kind of like that.

It took place in March 2022, and shortly afterward I had to

make the difficult decision to close down the DHM, as I am now living in Missouri to be closer to my family, and there is no one with the time or ability to carry it forward in Denver. Founding and working with the DHM was one of the best things the Lord ever asked me to do. Between our own street outings and doing the training the first two years of Christ in the City, working with a fantastic outreach team, and meeting, loving, and making many homeless friends along the way has been amazing. Yet it was time to move on and deep in my heart I knew that. I am still so grateful to everyone who was a part of this ministry at one stage or another, it has truly touched my heart and will stay with me forever.

Although I didn't plan it this way, I think it was almost meant to be that I came to this decision after the March 2022 trip. That trip set the stage perfectly for what I believe God is asking and inviting the people who have been associated with the DHM and the Rome trips to do for the future.

When God Has Other Plans

As the COVID-19 lockdowns and bans on international travel began to wind down, I immediately knew I wanted to do another trip, but that 2021 would be impossible. It was just too soon, and too many things were up in the air still, so I started looking at dates for 2022, and finally settled on March 2–9 for this trip.

Before I even really started planning or thinking about the trip in any real way, I felt deep in my heart that if I was going to lead another trip, Shyla was the person who was meant to go, again. Given her last experience in Rome and the transformation that has taken place in her since, I truly thought she deserved a second chance. I hoped she could see Rome through different eyes and experience it without all of the anger that she had been holding onto which got in the way of really enjoying the last visit. She was doing better with her health too, so it seemed the time was right. An anonymous donor, who knew about Shyla's story and was also convinced that she deserved the second opportunity, decided to pitch in $1200 so she could experience Rome through the lens of her new attitude and Christian faith. I decided to match that $1200 myself so I didn't have to fundraise, because I hate fundraising.

Rachel was of course going to be the chaperone for this trip again, and I promised to get her name right on the reservation this time around, which, miraculously, I did! I also offered Cassi the opportunity to come on this trip, since she missed out on seeing so many things when she went in 2020.

Along the way I also decided to bring a woman I met named Patti Fairbank, who was seventy-five. I met Patti when she came into the Women's SafeHouse Thrift Shop where I work one day, and we started chatting. In the course of the conversation, I told her about the Rome trips, and Patti said she'd give anything to have the opportunity to do something like that, because she had never really traveled. Patti told me she had raised thirteen foster children, and buried some of them, and had never really had many opportunities to do things for herself, including travel. I immediately felt a tug in my heart telling me she was supposed to come with us, but since none of us knew her, I thought I'd better ask the girls before making the offer. Well, I explained the situation and the response was overwhelming — Patti was going to come with us, and she was absolutely overjoyed when I told her she would be included on the trip!

From the beginning, I told Rachel that I would pay for her airfare, in part to make up for my mistake the last time, but in the end, I made her pay some of it because everyone sent their information in late and by that time the cost had gone up. I also paid for part of Cassi's airfare, but Patti paid for her entire trip herself, and she also paid for most of the taxis we took in Rome, as we hadn't included taxi fares in the pricing but she didn't feel that she could walk from place to place like the girls could.

Planning this trip in many ways was no different than any other trip I've taken, but the questions, concerns, and unknowns surrounding travel protocol and COVID-19 testing requirements were difficult for all of us. I ended up using a mail-in test kit that cost me thirty-nine dollars and I had my certificate for a negative result within fifteen minutes. Patti ordered hers but had problems with the video, so she went to a Walgreens and had it done there. Rachel got hers done at the airport for a whopping $255. I'm not sure where Cassi had hers done, but everyone managed to get theirs done — right down to the wire!

I had given everyone a deadline for when to send me a copy of their passport and basic personal information. That part is always a hassle, and sure enough, this time there was also a hiccup because Patti discovered her passport had expired and needed to get an expedited replacement at the last minute, but she did manage to get it in time! After flights were purchased, I secured our Airbnb apartment and bought tickets to Florence and Assisi, and we were ready to go. Or so I thought.

Well, it was only a few hours after I had purchased the train tickets and booked a couple of tours that Shyla called me. She was in the hospital and had to have emergency surgery for a brain bleed but was still going to try to make it on the trip. Now, this was only a few weeks before we were supposed to leave, and I knew brain surgery would take longer to heal from than that. She had over forty stitches, and had to reacquaint herself with basic functions afterward, so I pleaded with her to ask her doctors and her adoptive mom before making any decisions. They all told her no, that it just wouldn't be possible, so she reluctantly agreed to stay.

Shyla was very disappointed when that happened, and I was too. We all wanted her to have this trip and to have a second shot at enjoying the Rome experience, so it was hard on everyone who knew her and knew how much she'd been looking forward to going. I know Shyla wanted so badly to prove how much she had changed, and that this trip was her opportunity to do that, but I don't think that's needed and I've told her that. I plan to return to Rome on my own in October 2022, and I hope to bring Shyla with me then, if she's well enough to travel, but three things have to happen first: Her doctors need to give her a 100 percent release to go, airfare costs need to go down, and the insurance company we used for this last trip needs to refund me the money for her airfare this time, since her reasons for not going were health-related.

The difference in Shyla is so dramatic; day and night from the person she was when I took her to Rome five years ago. She's very humble, and sometimes she's way too apologetic for her past actions. Once I'd forgiven her, I was done, and the more she keeps bringing it up the more I keep remembering some of the really awful things she said and did, and I'd just prefer for her not to. I want to remember her as the person she is today: warm, loving, kind to everyone, and she always has a smile on her face, even when she has tears in her eyes. That's who I see her as, and that's the person I want her to see when she looks at herself. While she was disappointed not to go, she didn't need Rome to help her do that. I think she's still on an incredible journey that we're only seeing the beginning of, and I do hope that a second experience of Rome is still in her near future.

A Bumpy Arrival

Shyla pulling out at the last minute was only the first of several things that did not go according to my carefully set plans for this trip. Once she told me she wouldn't be able to go, we went ahead and made the calls we needed to, but moved forward with planning for the rest of the group as usual. Patti and I arrived in Rome two days ahead of the other girls, but because we had to wait to buy plane tickets while her passport was being renewed, the only decently priced itinerary we could get took us through what felt like an eternal voyage with stops in four countries: the United States, Canada, Germany, and finally Rome. It wasn't as bad as it sounds, and it was definitely an adventure! The only real problem we had, other than Patti getting a sore back, was filling out the documentation finder that was required in order for us to fly. It took several people at different airlines to help us figure out how to do it, but finally a millennial flight attendant from Air Canada got it done and man, was that a relief!

By the time Patti and I arrived at our Airbnb, which was huge, we took some time to put our stuff in our rooms and then went on what I thought would be a little walk to fill our refrigerator with wine, cheese, and snacks. Of course, that walk took three hours because I ended up getting lost and couldn't navigate us back to our apartment, even though the marketplace was literally a few blocks straight down from where we were staying. The problem is that we went out a wrong door, and I got confused. When I say that I'm directionally challenged, I'm not kidding! That was another "blooper" that didn't quite pan out the way I expected. This is one of the many reasons why Rachel goes with me on these trips.

The next day we met Elise and her husband John at the Wisdomless Club, which I love, for cocktails. Of course, we decided to walk there, because I am used to walking everywhere we go in Rome, but it ended up being way too much for Patti. Between the lengthy trip over and the three-hour walk the night before, she was having muscle spasms and had put her hip out and was in a lot of pain. Elise had gotten us tickets for the pope's Wednesday general audience the next day, and we were supposed to meet the pope as the other girls were arriving, but Patti just couldn't do it, so Elise set up a massage for her. After a ninety-minute massage, Patti still had trouble, but she was a lot better and was able to function the rest of the trip because of that.

Although I was disappointed that we didn't get to see the pope due to yet another unexpected change of plans, it all worked out really well in the end because the girls' flight got in, and we were able to let them into the Airbnb right away so they could get settled in. Then we all met Patti after her appointment and headed to the Vatican Museums, where Patti and Cassi had a tour. When we were signing up for the tours, it was a little iffy as to whether Rachel would be able to go because she had not had her COVID booster shot. I believe that requirement was dropped the day we got there, but it worked out because Rachel and I have been to the Museums many times before, so we were able to just walk around and enjoy ourselves while Patti and Cassi were inside. We met up with them once they were done and wandered around for a while before going back to the Airbnb.

Going with the Flow

The rest of the trip was fun, but exhausting, as I had packed a lot into our itinerary. Since we'd come all that way, I felt I had to fit as much as possible into our time in Rome, and sometimes it was just too much, especially for Patti, who sometimes would choose to stay behind while the rest of us went out so she could rest and do things at her own pace. I really had to learn to let go and accept that it was okay for people to opt out of things and to go at their own pace instead of strictly adhering to the entire schedule. It stressed me out to leave people behind, as I felt responsible and wanted to make sure they were taken care of and got the full experience they wanted out of the trip, but in the end, I think everything worked out.

As usual, our day trip to Assisi was a big highlight for everyone. It's always amazing. We took it slow because there are a lot of hills and Patti's back was still sore, but everyone had a great time. Patti and Cassi are not Catholic, so they weren't as interested in all of the churchy stuff in Assisi, and since Rachel and I have been there and seen most of that before, we focused on doing what they wanted, and ended up just walking around and enjoying the city, which was nice, and I think was enjoyable for everyone. Of course, on the way back we missed our stop and had to get off at the next one, where we waited for forty-five minutes to get the train heading back to Assisi, but which stopped in Rome. There were quite a few sketchy people on the platform, and Cassi and I spent much of our wait trying to mentally decide what we would do if they attacked. It was funny and weird at the same time. In the end, we made it back alright, despite our detour.

The next day we were able to take the Scavi tour, below the Vatican, and we also visited St. Peter's Basilica and the Pantheon, finishing the day with dinner at Elise and John's place. Cassi remembered the meal John made for her and Angelique in 2020 and could not wait to sit and enjoy their beautiful terrace, which has two statues overlooking the street and is pretty much the most Roman terrace in the city! At least, that I've seen. Just being able to sit with friends and dine with "locals" was a big highlight. I think the girls felt special and spoiled to have someone go to the trouble of preparing a nice meal like that just for them. We were also able to meet someone I'd wanted to for some time: Mountain Butorac, who runs The Catholic Traveler travel company, and his wife Christina, who joined us for dinner. I've been following Mountain on social media for a long time and was excited to be able to pick his brain for tips on future trips.

We had to be up early the next morning to go to Florence, so it was a short night, and Patti decided to stay back as she preferred to have an easy day at the apartment and walk around at her own leisure. The rest of us got up before dawn and headed to Termini station. We had a wonderful time in Florence, looking around and exploring the little shops in the center of town. Cassi was excited to see Michelangelo's famous David statue there, so she went in to do that while Rachel and I took a break at a small café until she was out. It was a wonderful experience and although it was a long day, I think the girls appreciated it. In the end, it was probably a good thing that Patti hadn't joined us that day because, big surprise, we missed the Rome stop on our way back and got off in Naples, but because we were on the late train, there were no others that night, so we ended up staying at a hostel and got up very early the next morning to take the 5:00 a.m. train back to Rome! I don't think I've had so many "senior moments" at any other time in my life as I did on this trip. It was embarrassing to get the girls stuck after missing our stop, again, but it all sort of worked out and the girls took it like champs — they saw it as an adventure and it ended up being a fun deviation for us that we laughed about later — much later, after we got back to our apartment and went back to bed for a few hours!

Everyone's favorite day was a day trip to Anzio, a coast town about an hour outside of Rome on the train. This was a surprise for the group. I wanted to have one day where I completely surprised and spoiled them, so I did some research and asked around for a place close to Rome that was beautiful and would make an easy day trip, and Anzio is what I ended up with. I didn't tell them what we were doing that day, so I hurried them onto the train and when we got off, we explored the city and spent the day walking on the beach. Anzio is also near a large American military cemetery where some seven thousand nine hundred US servicemen and civilians are buried, most of whom died during the Second World War. Although we didn't actually know that at the time we visited Anzio, it was cool to think that we were so close to it. If I ever go back to Anzio in future trips, which I probably will, this will definitely be on the schedule.

One of best parts of that day for the group was walking on the beach, especially for Cassi — she had never been to a beach before and absolutely loved it! We had one of the best lunches I think I've ever had in Italy there, with the freshest seafood and the best wine. I'd go back to Anzio for the food alone!

We drew hearts for Shyla in the sand and sent her pictures, since she couldn't be there herself, and because one of her favorite things to do is to collect random hearts from the places she goes. I think that meant a lot to Shyla, and I truly hope that she is well enough to come with me on the next trip, so she can draw the hearts on the beach herself!

For the rest of the trip, we did the usual stuff: visiting the bone church, hitting up street shops, and going to the Colosseum. Since there were still so many COVID restrictions in place for getting into and out of the Colosseum, on when and how to get a ticket, and protocol for being inside, we decided to just walk around outside of it and take pictures without going in. We didn't do as many "churchy" things on this trip, which I missed, especially visiting a Paulist parish that I've come to really love, but this trip wasn't for me, and I think the group really enjoyed the things we did do.

There really were not meltdowns this time, in the classic sense that people have had them in the past, and I think that was in part because the dynamics of our group. The only real "meltdowns" happened when poor Patti hurt her back, and there was one night when Rachel and Cassi decided to go to a bar while Patti and I stayed in, and ended up overdoing it a bit. That wasn't really a meltdown, but it is not something I will allow to happen again. I'm glad they had fun, and I don't think they meant to overdo it, but it ended up causing problems the next day when the girls wouldn't get out of bed and spent half the day hungover! Our whole schedule for the morning had to be rearranged. I generally don't like to police people on these trips, but I decided that from here on out, no more bar outings — if people want to drink, they can do it at the apartment or when we're out for dinner, but I won't allow any more late-night outings like this, because it can affect the entire group. Cassi also struggled a lot with anxiety before and during the trip, and she has many ways that she deals with it to keep it under control. I just hope she is able to overcome that in her future — Cassi's had a tough life, and anxiety can be crippling, but I trust that no matter what's going on, God is working in her life, and I do believe these trips are having an impact on her. Whatever that is, I don't know and maybe I never will, but I trust that the Lord knows what he's doing!

When it came time to leave, we all flew out on the same flight from Rome to Newark. Rachel and Cassi headed back to Denver from there, and Patti and I waited for our connection to Chicago. It was of course delayed, so we didn't get in until 3:00 a.m. We stayed in a hotel that night, which was very relaxing, and sleeping in a decent bed that night was the perfect setup for the last part of the journey.

Looking Forward

As much as I enjoyed this trip, and I believe we all did, I would not want to repeat it again. I believe Rachel and Cassi formed a special bond and that Cassi found an ally in Rachel, but I came away realizing just how much I am lacking in mercy. I believe, for my part, that I should've had more mercy, love, respect, and compassion for Patti, who has gone through so much in her life and who was in pain for a good portion of the trip. Instead I found myself being annoyed at a lot of little things that she just couldn't help. Maybe what I saw in her reminded me of things I saw in myself and just didn't want to see, but I should have done better, and I wish I had in the moment. Getting annoyed at stuff along the way is part of leading any trip, but with this one in particular, I really saw how much I need to grow in my ability to be compassionate toward others, so maybe this trip was for me too, in that regard. I know that's something I'll be working on for next time!

So much of this trip was experienced not in following the

carefully crafted itinerary I had made, but in responding to the unexpected twists and turns that popped up along the way and finding adventure and joy even in a change of plans or a deviation from what we had in mind. These were the moments that really defined the trip, in a way, and we all had a better time because of them. At least, that's what I tell myself, since most of them were my fault! But I do think there is something providential about all these "bloopers" or mishaps happening on the last trip, because I think it helped prepare me for the next stage in all of this.

Usually, the trips have been for a specific individual, and that was clear from the moment that person was laid on my heart — there was no doubt about who the Lord wanted to go — but this time, the person I really felt should go on the trip wasn't able to. So I've come to believe that this trip wasn't about any one person, but something else, something bigger, especially now that the DHM is coming to an end.

In some ways, I think this trip was for me, to show me how much I need to grow in mercy, but also to learn obedience to God's will. I do not believe this trip was for Cassi, Patti, or even Rachel, although it was important to all of them and it did help Rachel and I learn to work together better, which will be important in the future for people who have always wanted to do the Rome trips. I suppose it's inevitable when you do something like this, but I've found that some people who weren't selected got jealous, and there were others who weren't homeless but who were, in a sense, also jealous that they weren't able to go, and that it was something that was just offered to the homeless. What I've done through these trips, and especially this last one, I believe, is prove to people that they can have this experience themselves if they want it, and they can do it at an affordable price, if they know when and where to look for deals.

I truly believe that there's another life God wants to change out there, and that's why these trips aren't ending with the DHM, but are continuing with other people who might need them but can make it on their own, people who have seen these trips happen for the past eight years and who now know that it is possible, and that it is something they too can have if they want. For each of the people DHM has selected, they've seen that good things can happen to people in bad circumstances, and I think with Cassi, they've seen that they don't need to be invited to have that experience, but that drive and determination are enough. I think knowing that they can do this on their own if they want is also important, especially now that the DHM-sponsored trips are ending. This is something the Lord has laid on my heart very strongly, and I think that's why he's keeping me healthy, active, and alive.

Going forward, I know for certain that while the days of the DHM are coming to an end, this isn't the end of the story: It's just the beginning of another chapter! More lives will be changed by an experience in Rome — I'm confident of that. This is something I've prayed about and struggled through. I even went to the Marian shrine in Perryville, Missouri to pray about it, which, trust me, is something I never do, or have ever done! When I go to Rome again in October, it will be on my own, not through the DHM, to spend time in prayer and to regroup my thoughts for another trip in March 2023, where there will be ten people in the group, including Rachel's mother and two of her sisters. I have no idea why, but I really believe that somebody's life in this next group will be changed.

I do know beyond a shadow of a doubt that the Lord is not done with the "Rome trips" — they might look a lot different from here on out, but I'll still go, and the purpose is still the same: to restore dignity to those who are struggling.

Shyla may yet have the chance to go back. I initially thought this last trip was for Shyla, and it was, but in a way, it was for everyone, for all of my street friends, and for anyone who needs it. In a sense, that's the best legacy I could leave with these trips: not only to show people in difficulty that change is possible and that dreams are attainable, but that they don't need a handout to achieve them. They are able to realize these dreams on their own, if they believe in themselves and really desire the changes that are necessary to attain them. I don't know what God has planned or what he will do for the people who come on these trips in the future, but I do know with confidence that as I close the DHM chapter, a whole new story is beginning, and I can't wait to see where it takes me!

Conclusion

I once read in a book called *Do Something Beautiful for God*[*] a quote from Mother Teresa that I found to be perfectly suited to my ministry with the homeless. Mother Teresa said, "To know the problem of poverty intellectually is not to understand it. It is not by reading, taking a walk through the slums, that we come to understand it. We have to dive into it, live it, share it."

We will never really or truly understand the problem of poverty just by walking through the streets downtown or doing a drive-by of places that homeless people stay. We have to go a step further, get to know the names and faces of the needy in our communities, and find concrete ways to help, no matter how big or how small. Mother Teresa certainly dove in and not only embraced poverty but found God and her life's purpose through

---

[*]Mother Teresa and Matthew Kelly, *Do Something Beautiful for God: The Essential Teachings of Mother Teresa* (North Palm Beach, FL: Blue Sparrow Books, 2019).

it. Her life and vocation were unique, and her selfless love and generosity gained the admiration of the world. Yet not everyone is able to serve the poor in the slums of India, or take homeless people to Rome — in fact, I'm sure that I'm probably the only person crazy enough to do that! But there is a way for everyone to help. I am convinced that each and every person is capable of making a difference, once they find the way that's right for them. This can be done in a thousand different ways, and sometimes, as has happened with me, you might be surprised to learn that those who need our help aren't just the homeless.

If you are serious about wanting to do something, about wanting to make a difference or give back in some way, there are plenty of opportunities. Some of the main questions people have when they are first getting started in homeless ministry are pretty basic: How do I help? How and where do I get involved? Is it appropriate to give money? If so, how and when? These and many other questions can all seem overwhelming at first, but the more you do, and the more experience you gain, the clearer the answers to these questions become. I personally don't have a defined "code" that I follow, a set list of dos and don'ts; I simply let God lead me — I follow the little tugs on my heart, and let myself respond to the needs in front of me, and the invitations I believe God is making. I know that might not sound very helpful, so I've compiled a list of some experiences and best practices I think might be of use to anyone wanting to get involved in this kind of ministry.

Diving In

When I first got involved in homeless care in my Denver neighborhood, it was a matter of just showing up. The Cathedral Basilica of the Immaculate Conception downtown, the parish I often attended, issued a call one day for volunteers to help pass out "snack packs" in front of the church every weekday afternoon

4:00–4:30 p.m. I signed up, and I found out it was a great way to break down some of the Colfax stereotypes and get to know some of the people who hang out at the bars or on the corners. Many of them are alcoholics or drugs users and dealers who hang out on every corner. They really seemed to look forward to the water, fruit, crackers, and Slim Jims we handed out. Many families who live in some of the low-income high rises in the area will send their kids to get a few snack-pack bags on handout days to put in their lunch bags for school.

We heard many stories of men and women who in their younger days had families, worked decent jobs, and were extremely happy until some tragedy happened which caused them to lose everything. The thought of themselves and their families being homeless was just too much to bear so they turned to alcohol or drugs for relief and got hooked. Now, they struggle just to buy the alcohol or drugs they need to sustain their habit, and to find a place to lay their heads where they can feel safe. Many are beaten up beyond recognition in the night and their meager belongings have been stolen. Women tend to find a man to attach themselves to for safety, warmth, and some resemblance of love. This "love" almost always turns out to be a farce, a counterfeit love, as Pope St. John Paul II would say. They are often raped, beaten, and lose the little hope they were holding onto. The few that make it are very small in number. There simply are not enough treatment centers to accommodate those who have fallen through the cracks.

I tried as best as I could to help these people through the various organizations I got involved with, but when I eventually established my own ministry, we sought to fill some of these gaps, and we do the best we can to meet the immediate basic needs of those we meet on the streets, whether it's food, clothing, socks, or much-needed toiletries like tampons, toothpaste, and a toothbrush. Those are often the most useful items you can give, if you are looking to donate something. I can't tell you how many women we've met on the streets who are grateful to have some feminine care items for a month.

Giving Money

Some people who want to help the homeless think that giving them money is the only way to do that. Others want to help but refuse to give money because they don't want it going toward drugs or alcohol, but toward something that would actually help. I myself have flip-flopped on this a bit during my time working on the streets.

For years, I believed and taught volunteers that you should never give homeless people money, as I assumed it would not be used for any good purpose. After some time, I came to understand that this belief stemmed from my own expectations of how the money ought to be used. Then one day I heard the story of a priest named Fr. Charles Woodrich, lovingly known as "Father Woody," who became Denver's "patron saint of the poor." He once famously said, "No one wants to go down and live under a bridge the rest of his life. Something happened, and when that something happens, we lose something within us. That's why we need one another." Not only did Father Woody set up shelters, with computer and phone hook-ups, showers, and a laundry facility, but he also randomly handed out twenty-dollar bills, which is a Christmas tradition the Cathedral of the Immaculate Conception continues to this day. It is estimated that between seven hundred and one thousand four hundred homeless people attend the event, which begins with Mass, and afterwards envelopes with Father Woody's image and twenty dollars cash inside are given to each individual who attends. Not one person is asked how they are going to spend this money.

After much prayer and soul searching, one year I decided to put aside fifty dollars in five-dollar bills to randomly hand out on the street — not just to homeless, but to anyone I felt the Lord lay on my heart. Anyone. This was a huge step for me because I didn't have that much money at the time, and just randomly giving it away went totally against the grain of my heart, and of my wallet! It was also difficult for me because it conflicted with my previous ideas, beliefs, and principles; it meant I had to betray my own teachings, but since I felt like it was the Lord who was asking, I did it.

I then had a series of random experiences and encounters over the following month that I believe were inspired by the Lord, and which also helped change my perspective. I remember that somewhere along the way, I had been sick with the flu for a week, which was a rarity for me, when finally I ventured out for more Kleenex, supplies, and my favorite indulgence: an ice cream cone from the McDonald's on Colfax. While I was out, I came across three young high school students entering McDonald's at the same time as me. Two of the young men were placing their order when the third walked in, and they were shocked because he wasn't ordering anything. When the young man said he was broke, the other two boys asked him why he didn't get money from his dad, and he simply replied, "I'm fine, and I'll just hang out." These were not homeless kids, so I was confused by the tug I felt in my heart. Yet, I listened to that wee little voice and as I walked by the young man and his friends, I placed a folded up five-dollar bill next to his hand and walked out, feeling elated that I had followed my gut, yet eager to remove myself. I was in the middle of thinking or rethinking about what the Lord was asking when the young man ran out of McDonalds and chased me down the street shouting, "Lady, lady, is this OK? Is this for real?" I said, "Sometimes not only the homeless need a lift." He responded, "Lady, you totally made my day, maybe even my year. Nobody has ever just given me something for just being." Then he gave me a very tight hug before going back inside. Random acts of kindness can mean so much more than you can imagine. Let the Lord lead you!

Another time, one of my homeless friends was sitting at a table on the 16th Street Mall when I was walking by. He yelled at me to come over and meet his brother, who had just gotten to Denver. I found the brother had just jumped off the train; many summer homies are "rail riders" who hop on and off trains at different cities. He was toting a guitar and looked pretty beat and sad. I asked him if he was OK and glad to be with his brother. He said he hadn't eaten in several days and was so hungry that he could eat his guitar at this point. As I was leaving, I laid a five-dollar bill beside each of the young men, which caused my friend to jump up, totally confused, and shout, "Thank you!" He told his brother that I never ever hand money out, so his brother made the comment, "You must really be special to her." I told him not to spread the word, because I had only fifty dollars to last the entire month.

I still don't know how I personally feel about just giving cash, but if the Lord asks you to do this, then do it and don't worry about being judged. Let him lead you! Bottom line here is, money is definitely not the only way to help, nor is it the main way, and I don't think it should be. But there are times when it is appropriate. It just depends on the circumstance, and you'll be able to judge that better for yourself with time and experience.

Help Is More than Money
Even though I am more open to handing out cash than I was, if I truly see a need, that is definitely not the only way to help. Even the smallest actions can make a difference.

This was driven home for me one night while I was on my way home from work and decided to stop at a grocery store to pick up a few items. I passed by the deli to buy a handful of popcorn chicken to munch on for the rest of the way home. At the time, I worked a full-time job pushing wheelchairs at the Denver International Airport, and after getting off work late from the airport and with an hour drive back home, I was exhausted and hungry. The lady behind the counter kept dropping things and apologizing, saying she had a lot on her mind. I was getting impatient but told her it was okay and there was no rush. Then she looked at my hand and said she liked the ring I was wearing, which was a pretty ring with bright red rubies. It looked real, but I had found it in a drain by the river, so I was pretty sure it wasn't. After checking out, I reached over the counter and laid the ring next to her hand and said, "Hope your day is better." She didn't just tear up, she started crying, and thanked me over and over again. So, the moral is: Pay it forward, and don't stop to count the cost. It's so much fun that way! Let the Lord lead you.

When I was working at the airport in Denver, I would meet people from all walks of life. I remember one afternoon: As I was getting ready to go through security to get to the concourse so I could meet an incoming plane, I bumped into a man asking for directions. I knew he was homeless, not so much because of his looks, but by the story he was telling me as I walked with him to the security line. As I walked with him, I could see that he was anxious, so I took a little time to walk and talk with him to help calm his anxieties, especially before he boarded a plane. He told me his estranged daughter found him on Facebook and was flying him to California so she could see him and introduce him to her family. It was hard for me not to tear up. I smiled and told him he should probably comb his hair, because it was pretty untidy. His response was, "They get me as I am!" Well, I smiled back and said, "Maybe you could let them see you as you want to be, and not as you are labeled." He was silent for a few seconds, and then asked where he could buy a comb. Then I really teared up! Maybe if we didn't spend so much time judging others, we could actually help and make a difference! Let the Lord lead you.

Have you ever been or wondered if you were being tested by the Lord? And have you ever seen the results of that test within minutes? Well, that has happened to me, and as far as I know, I passed. One instance of this happened back in Denver. My apartment manager at the time cleaned out the apartments in my building when tenants moved out. Oftentimes, people leave many items behind when they go, including spare change. He finds lots of coins in sofa cushions, dresser drawers, and money jars that have been left behind by people who choose not to fully clean out their apartments. When this happens, he just puts the items and coins on the curb by the dumpster for anybody who comes by to pick through. He once offered a homeless man a drawer that was full of stuff and told him he could sort through it and take whatever he wanted. The man came back a few days later to thank him, because he had found $61 in change, which was enough to pay for a night in one of the better motels, where many homeless will stay so they can clean up and be warm for the night. On the day my apartment manager told me this, he said that he had just placed a lot of coins on the curb that he found in one of the units. He had taken the quarters out to use for laundry, so most of what was left were nickels and dimes, and a few pennies. When I went to look, I couldn't believe how much there was. After I finished talking with him, I went inside to get a coat so I could pass out Snack Packs at the Cathedral that afternoon, and when I came out, all the change was still there. With nobody around, my heart jumped, and my mind said, "Score!" I scooped up that change so fast it would make your head spin. I stuffed both my pockets so full they were bulging. There must have been eight to ten dollars just in dimes and nickels.

I walked to the street where we handed out snack items, and as I was waiting for the light to change to cross over, a woman approached me asking if I had any spare change. She was dressed nicely, and she showed me that she had about thirty cents in her pocket. I wondered why she could possibly need change if she was dressed so nice, so I asked her why she needed the money. There I went, judging someone by their appearance, as I was fingering the wads of change in my pockets! My immediate thought was that I wasn't about to give it up to someone dressed better than I was, but what the woman said took me by surprise. She said that she had never been homeless before but had hit hard times and just moved back into an apartment, but because she was paying rent now, she didn't have any money for food. The tears in her eyes and the quiver in her voice made me know in my heart that she was legit, and that asking for money was very new and hard for her to do. As I started emptying my pockets into hers, her eyes widened, and tears rolled down her face as she hugged me. I do believe I passed that test set in front of me, however reluctantly. I'm not broke, all my needs are currently met, and yet sometimes I remember my early days when I was raised in the projects and lived on the streets with nothing, and I simply forget to trust God for ALL my needs, wants, and desires. Let the Lord lead you.

Sometimes helping out doesn't mean giving money or anything at all, except for a smile or nod of the head. Melanie used to say that when she was "flyin' a sign" — something that reads "anything helps," or something like that — money was always appreciated, but more important than money or even food handouts was just being acknowledged, with a hello or a smile. Even that was enough to make a difference in her day — it was enough to make her feel human and visible to someone, even for a second, and some days, that's all that was needed. I've heard it said that a look can change a life. I never used to understand that. To me, the look of hate can scare, the look of fear can put you on guard, and the look of love can lead to mistrust. When people come from difficult situations, the looks they get can teach them to continue down a path of unbelief. At a certain point, I realized that I had done this myself during my time helping those on the streets. It takes a lot of love to break down all those fears we hold onto so tightly, but if we allow God to lead us, it's more than possible!

Change Starts with Yourself

I could go on and on — there are so many stories to tell of other people I've met, or the time I lived in a box for two days around Thanksgiving to raise awareness about homelessness and ended up comforting a woman who wasn't homeless, but whose brother died suddenly, and the family's Thanksgiving dinner was canceled, so she was all alone and accidentally ended up sharing our homeless Thanksgiving banquet! There are many miraculous and inspired things that have happened in my time doing this ministry, and so many ways in which I've seen God change people's lives, including my own. The stories are endless, as are the opportunities to help those in our midst.

When you see people several times a week, as you do in the ministries I've been involved in, they become close to you in special ways. They become family. You learn their stories, their ups and downs. You become a stable part of their lives, and they yours. When you have had this ongoing contact with them for months, or even years, their hurts become your hurts, and their joys become your joys. You are excited to see them, and to hear what they are doing to improve their lot in life and change their future. You cry with them in times of sorrow and rejoice in their successes. You accept them for who they are, and they do the same for you.

Oftentimes it's hard to know what you can do to truly help those on the streets, as the line between helping and enabling can be blurry. It's a topic I often wrestle with. I think we all have the hope of the shining white knight coming to our rescue, changing our lives, and setting us on a path of righteousness. Ultimately, this has already been accomplished by Christ's sacrifice on the cross, but we also believe that all of our experiences form us into the person God wants us to be. Maybe it's not necessarily the person we want God to make us into. After all, don't we all have dreams of grandeur? I mean, if God really cared, wouldn't we be an amazing person without any stress or pain in our lives, and who was capable of making it on our own? Yet, if we could take a step back, we could see that in him, we already are that amazing person, just the way we are. The stress in our lives so often is what we have created for ourselves because of our lack of trust.

I believe people on the streets to some extent know this, but they can't make the rest of us see what they see, which must be very frustrating for them. They have a bigger family than most of us would ever dream of having. A family who watches out for them, who has their back in every situation, who tells it like it is, corrects, admonishes, and loves them fiercely. Once someone leaves the streets, it takes a long time to separate from their street family, and that can make it difficult for them to take the steps they need to in order to move on. They know it's best to limit or even cut ties, and that they must move forward, yet their past is often holding them down. We all have things in our own lives that we should release, but these things often have such a tight grip on us that we just can't move forward. Yet the Lord patiently waits for us to seek him so he can give us the desires of our hearts.

While I believe all of this firmly, I do not engage in direct evangelization through my ministry. I have found in working with people on the streets from all walks of life — young and old, men and women alike — that the one theme that constantly emerges is low self-esteem. In so many ways, they are no different than me. Nor are they any more ready to enter into a formal class on Church doctrine than I was when I was in their situation. My life and my actions must show the change I want to see in them. I had such a poor image of myself. Jesus was the love I was looking for, but I didn't discover that for a long time, so when I started this ministry, I knew that the people to whom I was ministering would not find Jesus' love through my words but through my walk and talk, in how I lived out the love of Jesus that filled me. I fail and I fall, more times than I can count, but I never give up on Christ because he never gives up on me.

Each step of the ministry the Lord has put me in is a prayerful step. I often argue with him over something I feel he's leading me to do, but in the end, I always say yes because somehow, it always comes out for the better. He guides me and brings all his ideas to fruition. What a joy it has been to follow Jesus. I never dreamed my life could be so full. My hope is that each and every single person who reads the stories in this book has the same experience of fullness and joy that I do in responding to God's endless invitations!

In Memory Of

Apache
Davon Gray
George "Teddy Bear" Saur
Eric Ornelas
Jeremy Peterson
Michelle Keller
Josh Mosh
Katie "Anything"
Mark "Pockets" Murphy
Michael Marchant
Jimmy Fingers
Nat
Jessica Daigle
Faith
Amanda "Sugarbear" Tourville

Ashley Romero
Binky
Brandon
Chuck
Jerome
Sean Watson
Richard Guerrero
Eddie
Nicholas Johnson
Daniel Webster
Mistika
Chico
Regina George Lintz
Angelina Montoya
Robin
Tiny
David
Trinity Smith
Lil Val
Brandon "Will" Cottle
Miguel Camacho
Weasel
Lil Wednesday
Ed Gates
Skitzo
Perry
Christina
Paige
Will
Daisy Smasie
Derrick "Tree" Yearout

Acknowledgments

First of all, I'd like to thank and praise the Lord for his unfailing love and guidance. A special thanks goes in particular to Elizabeth Lev for believing in these stories and getting the ball rolling for this publication.

I'd also like to thank everyone for their prayers and support — you are all truly amazing.

A very special thank you must go to: Fr. Michael O'Loughlin for his direction and guidance; Fr. Dave Dwyer for his unending belief if my adventures; Stephen & Alexandra Braunlich for all their support; Lane Andrews for the personal support he and his family have given to me; Chris Haas for all she has done for my homeless friends and for me; Perla and Mark for supporting the very first Homeless to Rome trips; Raquel Mora for being a chaperone on these trips — without her, I'd probably still be lost in Rome somewhere — Jeremy Revera for stepping in when others were giving up on the Homeless to Rome trips; Otis Anderson for always believing the Lord had a plan and I just needed to listen and trust; my family for their love and support throughout my entire life; Randy Erickson for helping the DHMs with a place to hold DHM events and continuing to reach out to the homeless on Capitol Hill; Jacob Starkovich, for getting our background checks done so we could plan all these trips without complications; Rachel Armendariz for being the DHM's VIP and outreach director; Chris Navarra for setting up our website and his mother Theresa for maintaining it; Deacon Price Hatcher III, for being our first treasurer and getting everything set up to run smoothly; Maureen McPadden for so much support to the homeless on the streets of Denver and for jumping in to helping fulfill individual needs with these trips when needed, and her daughter Rheala Melesio who was the DHM's communication director; and finally, to the amazing flight attendant who sends out emails whenever requested for support and updates of our trips.

If I've left anyone out, please forgive me — it was not intentional.

About the Authors

Tanya Cangelosi

Being very rebellious at a young age, and graduating from Concordia University at the age of thirty-four, gave Tanya the ability to see that good things can happen to anyone, even those who have nothing and believe they are not worth anything. Tanya believes everyone can fulfill their dreams if they truly believe in themselves.

Through working with the homeless on the streets of Denver, volunteering with the Missionaries of Charity to help orphans in Kolkata, and working at The Women's SafeHouse thrift shop in Missouri which benefits abused women, the Lord has given Tanya a deep love for the marginalized and an amazing opportunity to take eight homeless people to Rome from Denver.

The special love Tanya has gained for Rome will push her to continue leading trips to Rome, specifically helping people who have always dreamed of going, but never thought they could manage it. She shows them that whatever their means, it is attainable. She loves to wander the streets of Rome, often getting lost, but that doesn't stop her from coming back and giving others the opportunity to share her passions, which are Jesus and Rome.

Elise Ann Allen

Elise Ann Allen is a Denver native who currently works as a senior correspondent for the *Crux* news site, and is in Rome, covering the Vatican and the global Church. Before joining *Crux*, Elise worked with Catholic News Agency, first as a multimedia and content management assistant in Denver, and then as senior Rome correspondent covering the Vatican.

She graduated from the University of Northern Colorado in 2010 and holds degrees in philosophy and communications.

Her work with the homeless began in 2011, when she began doing outreach with Tanya and the DHM while contemplating entering religious life. She continued to follow the stories of her homeless friends after moving to Rome in 2013, reporting on each of the Rome trips, and she maintains friendships with Tanya and several of the homeless youth she met on the streets to this day.